TODAY'S RISING STARS: INSPIRING BASEBALL STORIES FOR YOUNG READERS

TRUE INSPIRATIONAL TALES ABOUT PERSEVERANCE AND COURAGE TO INSPIRE YOUNG BASEBALL LOVERS

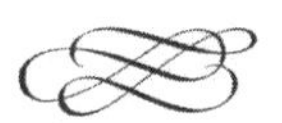

JORDAN ANDERS

CONTENTS

Introduction 7

1. AARON JUDGE 13
   - Aaron's Story 13
   - Aaron Judge Fun Facts 16
   - Things to Think About 17
   - Up Next 17
2. MIKE TROUT 19
   - Mike's Story 19
   - Mike Trout Fun Facts 23
   - Things to Think About 23
   - Up Next 23
3. SHOHEI OHTANI 25
   - Shohei's Story 25
   - Shohei Ohtani Fun Facts 29
   - Things to Think About 29
   - Up Next 29
4. FREDDIE FREEMAN 33
   - Freddie's Story 33
   - Freddie Freeman Fun Facts 36
   - Things to Think About 36
   - Up Next 36
5. JUAN SOTO 39
   - Juan's Story 39
   - Juan Soto Fun Facts 42
   - Things to Think About 43
   - Up Next 43

6. BRYCE HARPER 45
Bryce's Story 45
Bryce Harper Fun Facts 48
Things to Think About 49
Up Next 49

7. CLAYTON KERSHAW 51
Clayton's Story 51
Clayton Kershaw Fun Facts 54
Things to Think About 55
Up Next 55

8. MAX SCHERZER 57
Max's Story 57
Max Scherzer Fun Facts 60
Things to Think About 60
Up Next 61

9. PETE ALONSO 63
Pete's Story 63
Pete Alonso Fun Facts 66
Things to Think About 66
Up Next 67

10. JOSÉ ALTUVE 69
José's Story 69
José Altuve Fun Facts 72
Things to Think About 72
Up Next 72

11. JUSTIN VERLANDER 75
Justin's Story 75
Justin Verlander Fun Facts 78
Things to Think About 78
Up Next 78

12. RONALD ACUÑA JR. 81
Ronald's Story 82
Ronald Acuña Jr. Fun Facts 84
Things to Think About 84
Up Next 84

13. NOLAN ARENADO 87
Nolan's Story 87
Nolan Arenado Fun Facts 90
Things to Think About 90
Up Next 90

14. MANNY MACHADO 93
Manny's Story 93
Manny Machado Fun Facts 97
Things to Think About 97
Up Next 97

15. GERRIT COLE 99
Gerrit's Story 99
Gerrit Cole Fun Facts 104
Things to Think About 104
Up Next 104

16. MARCUS STROMAN 107
Marcus' Story 107
Marcus Stroman Fun Facts 110
Things to Think About 110
Up Next 110

17. MOOKIE BETTS 113
Mookie's Story 113
Mookie Betts Fun Facts 116
Things to Think About 117
Up Next 117

18. CODY BELLINGER 119
Cody's Story 119
Cody Bellinger Fun Facts 122
Things to Think About 122
Up Next 123
19. VLADIMIR GUERRERO JR. 125
Vladimir's Story 125
Vladimir Guerrero Jr. Fun Facts 128
Things to Think About 129
Up Next 129
20. GIANCARLO STANTON 131
Giancarlo's Story 131
Giancarlo Stanton Fun Facts 133
Things to Think About 133
Back to the Dugout 134
Conclusion 135
References 139

INTRODUCTION

Our story begins on a sunlit baseball field, the fresh scent of grass in the air, the mowers humming along, lines being painted, and bases being dusted off by the grounds crew. The game is set to begin in just a bit, and you feel a surge of excitement course through your bloodstream.

This feeling is what it's all about! This is baseball, America's favorite pastime—a sport that has captured the hearts of millions since the 19th century.

While baseball might not be as popular worldwide as soccer or basketball, it holds a special place in America. For generations, it has been a game of tradition, skill, and sheer love.

Records found in the National Archives tell us countless stories of baseball's role in American history, from the early days of racial integration to iconic World Series moments and even presidential first pitches.

A visit to the storied sanctuary that is the Baseball Hall of Fame in Cooperstown, New York gives us a good idea of baseball's deep significance in American culture. The enduring charm of the sport is deeply rooted in the American experience itself. Baseball stands for the values of teamwork, fair play, and athleticism.

Today, baseball is experiencing somewhat of a renaissance. Despite there being so many digital distractions, and entertainment options galore, the sport has seen a resurgence in popularity. Attendance at Major League Baseball games has surged recently, and with a few changes, the game has become more engaging than ever (Barkan, 2023).

New rules, like the pitch clock and limits on defensive shifts, have made the game faster and more exciting. Fortunately, for dedicated fans like us, the sport is reclaiming its place in the hearts of fans across the nation.

Baseball is more than just a game; it's a tradition that spans generations, bringing families and communities together. Parents across the country teach their kids how to throw a curveball, how to swing for the fences, and most importantly, how to love the game. This shared passion creates lasting memories and bonds that go beyond the sport and inform our lives.

Baseball offers many benefits: It teaches us how to work with others and rely on our teammates for support, and it offers us important lessons on the importance of cooperation. The gradual improvement in skills can boost our self-confidence and make it easier for us to overcome obstacles in life.

Baseball also improves our focus, gives us more patience, and increases our abilities in strategic thinking, all important skills both on and off the field. Additionally, it can help us build friendships and teach valuable social skills like sportsmanship and respect (*9*

Benefits of Playing Baseball for Kids, n.d.; *7 Benefits of Playing Youth Baseball*, 2022).

Every swing, every pitch, and every catch is an opportunity to improve and learn from mistakes. This helps us put on a growth-oriented mindset, one which favors long-term payoffs over short-term gain. The slow-paced nature of the game, even despite the recent time clock changes, helps us understand that effort, patience, and persistence are key to winning the game.

While it may lack some of the vigorous physical demands of sports like basketball and soccer, baseball promotes healthy physical development. Running the bases, swinging the bat, and fielding the ball all contribute to healthy levels of physical fitness. The sport encourages kids to be active, helping to combat the sedentary lifestyle that, unfortunately, is increasingly common among young people today.

In this book, we'll be exploring the lives of 20 contemporary baseball superstars. Their stories aren't just about these athletes' on-field achievements; they're also about the challenges these rising stars have overcome and how they've matured into well-rounded individuals.

We'll come face to face with players like Aaron Judge, whose leadership and determination have made him a standout star. We'll meet Shohei Ohtani, a marvel who excels both as a pitcher and a hitter, breaking new ground in baseball. And then there are athletes like José Altuve, who proves that size doesn't matter when you have the heart and will to succeed.

Each chapter will bring us a new story filled with exciting moments, interesting facts, and reflection questions to help you think about how these lessons apply to your own life. Whether it's learning about Bryce Harper's dedication or Ronald Acuña Jr.'s positivity, each story offers little tidbits of inspiration, hopefully helping you feel motivated and ready to chase your own dreams.

As you read these stories, imagine yourself in the players' shoes. Think about your own dreams and the qualities you need to achieve them. How can you show perseverance like Clayton Kershaw? Or embrace the changing tides like Mookie Betts? Each story offers a lesson that you can apply to your own life.

I'd encourage you to reflect on how these athletes have handled adversity, how they have remained focused on their goals, and how they've continued to push forward despite setbacks. These lessons aren't just for aspiring athletes but for anyone striving to achieve their dreams.

The reflection questions at the end of each chapter are designed to help you think deeper about the qualities that make these players successful. They encourage you to draw parallels between the players' experiences and your own life. What challenges have you faced, and how have you overcome them? What goals do you have, and what steps can you take to achieve them?

These questions are meant to inspire introspection and personal growth, helping you apply the lessons from these stories to your own interest in sports, and the other hobbies you pursue. Heck, thinking about these things might even help you out with problems at school, or at home!

So, get ready to dive into the world of tomorrow's baseball greats. These stories are here to entertain, inspire, and motivate you. Whether you're a budding baseball player yourself or are just a fan of the sport, there's something in these pages for everyone. Let the journeys of these amazing athletes remind you that with enough hard work, and the ability to dream, almost anything is possible!

As you turn the pages of this book, remember that every player featured throughout these chapters started just like you—as a kid with a dream. They faced challenges, doubters, and obstacles, but they never gave up. Their stories are proof that with dedication and perseverance, you can achieve your dreams too. Whether you aspire to be a professional athlete, a doctor, an artist, or anything else, the qualities these players embody—grit, endurance, and a positive attitude—are the universal keys to success.

Batter up! It's time to step up to the plate and get ready to be inspired. Let these stories fuel your passion and drive, and remember that every great journey begins with a single step. So, let's play ball and chase our dreams with everything we've got!

Chapter 1

AARON JUDGE

For me, it's just about taking it one at-bat, one pitch, one play at a time.

–AARON JUDGE

Aaron Judge is an icon of modern baseball, known for his powerful swings, his tall stature, and his epic home runs.

From his early days growing up in California, where he was adopted and raised by loving parents, Aaron developed qualities that helped propel him through his college baseball career and caught the attention of Major League scouts.

In this chapter, we'll look at the defining moments of Aaron's career, the challenges he's overcome, and the lessons his life path offers to young readers like you who dream of their own success in baseball and beyond. Let's learn Aaron's story.

AARON'S STORY

Aaron's path to baseball stardom was built on more than just natural talent. Born in Sacramento, California, he was adopted by Wayne and Patty Judge. Growing up in a supportive and loving environment, Aaron wasn't the only athlete in the family; his older brother, John, was also adopted, and the two boys shared a mutual passion for sports.

As a kid, Aaron played many different sports, including baseball, basketball, and football. But it was baseball that truly captured his heart. His impressive height and his natural athleticism set him apart.

Aaron's path to becoming a baseball superstar began when he went off to California State University at Fresno on a baseball scholarship. Throughout his college career playing with the Bulldogs, his talent was undeniable, and he quickly made a name for himself.

He earned several awards in college, including being named a first-team All-Conference player for three years in a row. His hitting was powerful, and his defensive skills were solid. He showed off his hitting power by winning the 2012 TD Ameritrade College Home Run Derby.

In 2013, Aaron's dream of playing pro ball finally came true! He got drafted by the New York Yankees. This marked the beginning of an exciting new chapter in his life. Signing with the Yankees, Judge received a whopping $1.8 million signing bonus (*Aaron Judge*, 2024).

His path to success in the major leagues was not easy though. He tore an upper leg muscle during practice, which benched him for his entire first season. Aaron's determination never wavered though. He used this time to prepare mentally and physically for his professional debut.

After recovering from his injury, Aaron spent several years honing his skills in the minor leagues before stepping onto the field with the Yankees. He played with the Charleston RiverDogs, impressing crowds with his powerful hitting and strong defensive play. His tour through the Yankees' various minor league teams also saw him playing for the Tampa Yankees and the Trenton Thunder, where he continued to develop his skills.

In 2016, Judge went on to play with the Scranton Wilkes-Barre RailRiders. His performance in the minors finally earned him a spot on the Yankees' roster, and on August 13, 2016, he finally made his major league debut against the Tampa Bay Rays. In his first game, he scored a whopping home run!

Aaron Judge's rookie season in 2017 was an awesome debut. He had a breakout season, hitting 52 home runs, setting a new rookie record, and was named the AL Rookie of the Year. His hitting abilities and impressive defensive skills quickly made him a fan favorite.

Aaron's awesome rookie season earned him a spot in the All-Star Game, and he won the Home Run Derby just like he did in college. He was the first MLB rookie to ever win the competition. His All-Star success was a clear indication that he was destined for greatness.

Since his debut, Aaron Judge has been a consistent performer, earning multiple All-Star selections and contending for the MVP award. His powerful hitting, combined with his leadership and work ethic, have made him one of the most respected players in the league.

Aaron's ability to lead by example, both on and off the field, has earned him the respect of other players and has gained him a loyal following of fans. His dedication to improving his game and his willingness to help his teammates succeed has solidified his status as a leader in the Yankees' clubhouse.

In the 2022 season, Aaron set a new American League record by scoring 62 home runs, breaking the previous record held by Roger Maris (*Aaron Judge*, 2024). His ability to consistently hit home runs and drive in runs made him a key player for the Yankees and a tricky opponent for the other team. Aaron's record-breaking season earned him the AL MVP award.

Despite dealing with injuries throughout his career, including a recent hit-by-pitch incident, Aaron Judge has shown strength. Each time he faced a setback, he worked tirelessly to come back stronger. Aaron's resilience has inspired countless young baseball enthusiasts to never give up, regardless of the challenges they face.

Off the field, Aaron is known for his charitable work through his ALL-RISE Foundation, an organization dedicated to providing fun, positive activities for kids like you to help keep you out of trouble. His commitment to giving back to the community and helping others is a reflection of his character and values. His charitable efforts have made a big impact, providing opportunities and support to young people in need.

As the captain of the New York Yankees, Aaron has become a leader both on and off the field. His leadership qualities, including his work ethic, humility, and dedication, have been notable. Aaron's ability to lead by example and his commitment to helping his team succeed have made him an invaluable asset to the Yankees.

Recently, Aaron again was included in the All-Star Game as a starter, continuing his streak of being a top vote-getter in the American League. His performance this season has once again demonstrated his incredible talent and dedication to the game.

AARON JUDGE FUN FACTS

- At 6'7" and 282 pounds, Aaron is the largest player to ever play the outfield position in MLB history.

- Aaron loves listening to Hip Hop and R&B, with favorites including Travis Scott, Drake, and J. Cole. He often DJs in the Yankees dugout, bringing music and a relaxed atmosphere to the team during practices.
- His favorite video game is *Fortnite*, and his favorite ice cream flavor is cookie dough.
- His favorite baseball movie is *The Sandlot.*

THINGS TO THINK ABOUT

- If you could hit a home run as far as Aaron Judge, where would you want it to land, and why?
- How would you encourage a teammate who is feeling down after a tough game?
- What big goal would you set for yourself if you were playing in the major leagues, and how would you achieve it?

UP NEXT

After tracing Aaron Judge's incredible path to baseball success, and understanding his impact both on and off the field, it's now time to turn to another rising baseball superstar who has also made waves in recent years: Mike Trout!

Like Aaron, Mike has found his way through the majors with his undeniable talent. As we learn about Mike's ride to the top of MLB glory, we'll see how he has consistently set new standards and become one of the most celebrated players in the game today.

ANGELS
27

Chapter 2

MIKE TROUT

I just keep thinking about putting up good numbers, playing hard and winning games.

–MIKE TROUT

From his early days growing up in New Jersey, to becoming one of today's top MLB superstars, Mike Trout's path to baseball stardom is a story of dedication, passion, and a strong commitment to the game. Known for his consistency and extraordinary talent, Mike's rise has been exciting to watch.

As we learn his story, we'll look at the milestones and challenges that have defined his path. His journey isn't just about the praise he's received or the records he's set; it's also about the perseverance that drives him to overcome obstacles and continuously strive for improvement. Mike's story is one of passion, hard work, and an authentic love for the game of baseball, making him a true inspiration for aspiring young athletes everywhere.

MIKE'S STORY

Born in Vineland, New Jersey, Mike was raised in the nearby town of Millville. From an early age, he loved the sport of baseball. Growing up, he played in the local Babe Ruth League, and by the time he was in high school, he was taking the sport to new heights. Mike's dad was Jeff Trout, who had a brief career in minor league baseball himself. Jeff undoubtedly had an influence on Mike's early love for the game, and he was very supportive of his son's growing passion for it.

In high school, Mike continued to refine his skills and wowed crowds at local games. He set a New Jersey state high school record by hitting 18 home runs in one season (*Mike Trout*, 2024). He led his team to numerous victories and managed to catch the attention of MLB scouts.

Mike's awesome performance in high school baseball led to him being selected by the Los Angeles Angels in the 2009 MLB Draft. Despite being a late first-round pick, Trout's potential was clear, and he quickly began to make a name for himself in the Angel's minor league affiliates.

Trout's ascent through the minor leagues was swift and impressive. He started his minor league career with the Arizona Angels, where he posted a .360 batting average (*Mike Trout*, 2024). His performance earned him a promotion to the Cedar Rapids Kernels.

By 2010, Mike was recognized as one of the top prospects in baseball, and his reputation continued to grow. He began to earn more recognition for his talents, including receiving the Topps Minor League Player of the Year Award. At just 19, he was the youngest player to ever win the award.

In 2011, Mike made his major league debut with the Angels. Although his initial stint in the majors was brief, he returned to the minor leagues with renewed determination and improved skills. By the next season, he was back in the majors and ready to make a lasting impact.

Mike's rookie season in the major leagues was, simply put, awesome. He finished the season with a .326 batting average, having hit 30 home runs and stolen 49 bases (*Mike Trout*, 2024). His excellent playing earned him the AL Rookie of the Year award. His combination of speed, power, and defensive ability quickly established him as one of the most thrilling players to watch.

Over the next few years, Mike's career started to soar. He won the AL MVP award three times: in 2014, in 2016, and then again in 2019. He quickly became a perennial All-Star, known for his consistency and all-around excellence.

Leading the American League in various offensive categories, Mike firmed up his reputation as being one of today's top players. His skills on the field were matched by his humble and hardworking demeanor, earning him respect from teammates, opponents, and fans alike.

However, Mike's journey has not been all fun and games. Injuries have periodically interrupted his career, including a knee injury in 2024 that required surgery. Despite these setbacks, Mike has always demonstrated resilience and a commitment to returning stronger.

Even in seasons where he got injured, Mike has managed to maintain an elite level of performance. From 2021 to 2023, despite spending a lot of time on the injured list, Mike still posted a .962 OPS and averaged 45 home runs per 162 games (Casella, 2024a).

The 2024 season started on a high note for Mike. He hit 10 home runs in the first 25 games, showing off his batting power (Bollinger, 2024). Unfortunately, he reinjured his knee in April, suffering another torn meniscus (a piece of cartilage in the knee), which sidelined him once more. However, his recovery has been promising.

Though he's been benched this season, Mike has been dedicated to his rehab regimen, working hard to regain his strength and return to the field. His commitment to training and staying in shape during his recovery period shows his dedication to the sport and his team.

As Mike continues blazing his path through MLB, he has some big career milestones ahead. At the time of this book being written, he's currently on the verge of joining the exclusive 400/200/50 club, which includes players who've managed to get 400 home runs, 200 stolen bases, and 50 triples. This achievement would place him among the legends of the game and further cement his legacy as one of the greatest players in baseball history!

Off the field, Mike's life is defined by a strong sense of family and personal interests. In 2017, he married his high school sweetheart, Jessica. Mike is passionate about fishing, hunting, and meteorology, hobbies that provide a balance to his intense professional life. His grounded personality and dedication to his roots have endeared him to fans and peers alike.

In 2014, President Barack Obama even mentioned Mike's name and his excellent playing in a speech he gave about the 2014 U.S. Farm Bill. This recognition from the highest level of government reflected Mike's influence beyond the baseball diamond, showing that his playing is inspirational to those in high positions of power.

Mike Trout's story is one about what can be achieved through talent, rigorous training, and hard work. From his early days in Millville to his current status as one of the game's greatest players, Mike has continually pushed the boundaries of what is possible. His path to baseball greatness serves as an inspiration to aspiring young ball players across the world.

As Mike continues to recover from his knee injury and prepares for his return to the field, fans and teammates eagerly await the next chapter in what has so far been an amazing professional baseball career.

MIKE TROUT FUN FACTS

- Mike likes to throw a ball into the stands between innings, creating fun for fans who are able to catch it!
- Mike has been selected for the All-Star team 11 times and has won nine Silver Slugger awards (*Mike Trout*, 2024).
- Mike loves football, hockey, and basketball too, and as a born-and-bred South Jersey guy, he proudly supports his hometown teams: the Eagles, the Flyers, and the 76ers.

THINGS TO THINK ABOUT

- Imagine you got a painful knee injury like Mike Trout. What creative ways would you stay involved with your team and continue to improve while you were getting better?
- Besides baseball, what hobby would you like to share with your fans, and how would you use it to connect with them?

UP NEXT

Mike Trout has blazed an amazing path to baseball success and has had a resounding impact on the game. His consistent excellence, record-breaking achievements, and strength in the face of challenges have inspired countless fans and aspiring athletes.

However, the story of modern baseball greatness doesn't end with Mike. Another player has captivated the baseball world with his unprecedented talents and dual-threat capabilities—Shohei Ohtani. Coming up next, we'll see how he's redefined what it means to be a superstar in Major League Baseball.

17

Chapter 3

SHOHEI OHTANI

I'm a student of the game, so I do feel like I need to grow every year, and I think I've been able to do that.

–SHOHEI OTANI

Shohei Ohtani's path, from a small town in Japan to the top of Major League Baseball, has been compelling to watch. Known as the "Japanese Babe Ruth," Shohei has redefined what it means to be a dual-threat player, excelling both as a pitcher and a hitter.

His levels of discipline, adaptability, and dedication to the sport have garnered him international fame, and have inspired countless fans and aspiring athletes around the world. This chapter is all about the life of Shohei Ohtani and his amazing capacity for excellence in multiple roles on the field. Let's learn Shohei's story.

SHOHEI'S STORY

Shohei was born in Oshu, Iwate, Japan, into a family that was deeply invested in sports. His dad, Toru, played amateur baseball in the Japanese Industrial League, and his mom, Kayoko, was a national-level badminton player.

Growing up with such top-notch athletic influences, Shohei was naturally interested in sports from a young age. He began to excel at a variety of sports. However, baseball quickly became his main focus. With Toru's guidance and coaching, young Shohei began to hone his skills. He soon exhibited an extremely high level of talent in the sport.

Shohei went to Hanamaki Higashi High School, where his talents on the baseball field quickly made him stand out from the other kids. Unlike many young athletes who might have chosen a prestigious baseball school in a major city, he opted to stay in his small village. His decision proved wise, as he flourished under the guidance of his high school coach, Hiroshi Sasaki.

By the time he was 17, Shohei was already setting records, including an insanely powerful 99 mph fastball that made scouts take notice. His performances in high school tournaments were legendary, combining powerful pitching with great batting skills. His high school career wrapped up with him having set records in Japan's prestigious high school baseball tournaments, making him designed to be a future star.

When he was 18, Shohei made his professional debut with the Hokkaido Nippon-Ham Fighters in Japan's NPB league. Many Japanese baseball fans eagerly anticipated his debut, and he did not disappoint. He played both as a pitcher and an outfielder, showing his versatility. At the end of his rookie season, he was chosen to play in the Pacific League All-Star team.

Over the next few years, Shohei continued to show off his awesome skills, leading the Fighters to a Japan Series championship in 2016. His ability to perform at an elite level both on the mound and at the plate made him a national sensation in Japan. He earned multiple All-Star selections and a few different awards, including the Pacific League MVP in 2016.

In 2017, Shohei made the big move to Major League Baseball (MLB), signing with the Los Angeles Angels. This move was highly anticipated and marked a big moment in baseball history. His ability to excel as both a pitcher and a hitter had not been seen since Babe Ruth.

Shohei's impact in his rookie MLB season in 2018 was revelatory. As a pitcher, he dazzled with a 3.31 ERA and 63 strikeouts over 10 starts (Augustyn, n.d.). His batting was equally impressive, with a .285 average, 22 home runs, and 61 RBIs (Augustyn, n.d.). These achievements earned him the AL Rookie of the Year award. Shohei's unique skill set captivated fans and analysts alike, establishing him as one of the most exciting players in baseball.

In 2018, things took a turn for the worse when Shohei needed a procedure called Tommy John surgery. Despite its name sounding cool, the surgery is actually quite painful. It's when pitchers get a torn ligament in their arm, and it needs to be repaired. The surgery meant that he'd be benched for the entire 2019 season.

As he began to recover and came back to the game, he focused on regaining his batting power. However, injuries continued to plague him, including a knee surgery in 2019 and a flexor strain in his right elbow in 2020. These setbacks tested Shohei, but he remained determined to return to full form. His commitment to recovery and improvement paid off, setting the stage for his historic 2021 season. Eventually, he made his way back to the mound.

The 2021 season was historic for Shohei. He became the first player ever to be selected for the All-Star team as both a pitcher and a hitter. Shohei finished the season with 46 home runs, 100 RBIs, and 156 strikeouts, leading the league in many different stats (Augustyn, n.d.). His performance earned him the American League MVP award, solidifying his place among the game's greats.

In 2024, Shohei signed a landmark 10-year, $700 million contract with the Los Angeles Dodgers, what was reported to be the largest contract in professional sports history (*Shohei Ohtani*, 2024). This move marked a new chapter in his career, underscoring his continued value and impact on the game.

Shohei's performance in the 2024 season has been phenomenal. Leading MLB in several offensive categories, including batting average, slugging percentage, and total bases, he has once again proved his capabilities.

His contributions have been a driving force for the Dodgers, proving his continued dominance and adaptability in the sport. Shohei's awesome season performance has solidified his reputation as one of the highest-performing players in baseball history.

Beyond his on-field achievements, Shohei is known for his charity efforts. In 2023, he donated tens of thousands of gloves to elementary schools all over Japan, aiming to inspire young children to take up baseball. His generosity and commitment to giving back have endeared him to fans worldwide.

Looking ahead, Shohei aims to help the Dodgers win a World Series. He continues to inspire fans worldwide with his unique talents and dedication to the sport. Shohei's journey from Oshu, Japan, to the top of MLB serves as a powerful reminder of what can be achieved with hard work, discipline, and an unwavering passion for the game.

Despite his fame, Shohei maintains a relatively private personal life. He is married to Mamiko Tanaka, a former professional basketball player. The couple keeps a low profile, valuing their privacy. Shohei also has a Kooikerhondje dog named Dekopin, who has been issued an honorary visa from the Embassy of the United States in

Tokyo. Shohei often attributes his success to his family's support and guidance. His personal life reflects his grounded and humble nature, which has endeared him to fans and teammates alike.

SHOHEI OHTANI FUN FACTS

- Shohei and Babe Ruth are the only players in MLB history to hit at least 10 home runs and win 10 games as a pitcher in the same season (Piccotti, 2023).
- Shohei often sleeps 10 or more hours a day and incorporates naps into his schedule to maintain peak performance. He even uses special custom pillows!
- His favorite baseball players include fellow Japanese stars Yu Darvish of the San Diego Padres and Hideki Matsui.

THINGS TO THINK ABOUT

- If you were a great pitcher and batter like Shohei Ohtani, which would be the place you feel most comfortable, on the mound, at the plate, or both?
- Imagine moving to a new country to play your favorite sport. Which country would it be, and why? If you moved to Japan, would you want to be a sumo wrestler or play baseball?

UP NEXT

Now that we've explored the incredible journey of Shohei Ohtani, let's turn our attention to another remarkable player who has made significant contributions to the game of baseball: Freddie Freeman!

Freddie's consistent playing, his leadership on and off the field, and the achievements he's realized over recent years have established him as one of the game's top first basemen. From his early days with the Atlanta Braves to his current tenure with the Los Angeles Dodgers, he's been recognized with multiple All-Star selections and a National League MVP award.

His impact on the game and the teams he's played for have been undeniable, making him one of the most influential players in modern baseball. Let's find out all about the life and career of Freddie Freeman and uncover what makes him such an important player in baseball today.

Braves

Chapter 4

FREDDIE FREEMAN

When you come back on top after you've fallen, it's a better story.

–FREDDIE FREEMAN

Freddie Freeman's path to baseball stardom has been a story of triumph and challenges. Freddie grew up with a deep-rooted love for the sport that, thankfully, was encouraged by his family. Despite coming up against barriers, he's continually risen to the occasion, meeting challenges head-on, while showing continued dedication and leadership.

Freddie's story is one of inspiration, marked by personal growth, professional achievements, and a profound love for the game. Let's learn Freddie's story.

FREDDIE'S STORY

Frederick Charles Freeman, or "Freddie," as he's known today, was born in Fountain Valley, California. His dad, Fredrick Sr., and his mom, Rosemary, were Canadians, living in the U.S. at the time of Freddie's birth, making baby Freddie eligible for dual Canadian and American citizenship.

Growing up in a baseball-loving family, Freddie's early life was deeply influenced by his mom, who instilled a strong work ethic in him, and a deep love for the game. He started playing baseball when he was just two years old. Tragically, his mom passed away from skin cancer when Freeman was only 10. This loss had a big impact on him. Freddie became determined to honor her memory through his achievements on the baseball field.

Freddie went to El Modena High School in Orange, California. He quickly established himself as a baseball prodigy on his school team. Playing both as a third baseman and a pitcher, he had a stellar senior year, hitting a .417 batting average and achieving a 6–1 win-loss record as a pitcher (*Freddie Freeman*, 2024). His performance earned him the local paper's Player of the Year award.

Recognizing Freddie's potential, the Atlanta Braves chose him in the second round of the 2007 MLB Draft. Though he had a college scholarship offer, he decided to sign with the Braves instead, beginning his professional baseball career and putting his academic ambitions on hold. His first stop after graduating from high school was making the rounds through various minor league teams.

Freddie's ascent through the minor league organizations was swift and impressive. He debuted with the Gulf Coast Braves in 2007 and progressed through the ranks, playing for the Rome Braves and the Myrtle Beach Pelicans. By 2009, Baseball America had ranked him as the Braves' fifth-best prospect. Even though he got a wrist injury that year, Freddie's talent and dedication were evident, leading to his major league debut in 2010.

The following season, Freddie secured his position as the Braves' starting first baseman. His rookie season was amazing, hitting .282 with 21 home runs and almost getting named NL Rookie of the

Year (*Freddie Freeman*, 2024). By 2013, he had his breakout season, earning his first All-Star selection and finishing in a solid fifth place in the MVP voting round with a .319 batting average, 23 home runs, and 109 RBIs (*Freddie Freeman*, 2024). His consistent performance led to a $135 million contract extension for eight more years (*Freddie Freeman*, 2024).

Freddie's career apex with the Braves came in the 2020 season when he won the NL MVP award. Despite the challenges of a pandemic-shortened season, Freeman led the Braves to the playoffs with a .341 batting average and an impressive 1.102 OPS (*Freddie Freeman*, 2024).

In 2022, Freddie signed a $162 million contract with the Los Angeles Dodgers for six years, marking the end of his 12-year tenure with the Braves (*Freddie Freeman*, 2024). His impact on the Dodgers was immediate, leading the team in several offensive categories. By 2023, he continued to excel, maintaining a high batting average and on-base percentage, and starting the 2024 season strong with highlights, including a grand slam against the Arizona Diamondbacks.

Freddie honors the memory of his mom by always wearing a long-sleeved shirt during games, something that can help prevent the development of melanoma, the kind of skin cancer she died from. Deeply involved in melanoma research and fundraising in honor of his mother, Freddie takes sun protection very seriously and wants to spread the message about using sunscreen and covering your skin, so cover up!

Be cool, and stay out of the sun when it gets too strong! If you're going to be exposed to strong sunlight playing baseball, or doing any other outdoor activities, don't worry, that's okay. Just make sure to wear a hat, load up on sunscreen, and always make sure to re-apply it throughout the day, especially if you get wet or sweat a lot.

Freddie's personal life and personal choices reflect his commitment to his family and community. He's married and has three sons of his own. Freddie wants to be around to spend time with kids like his mom didn't get to do. So be cool, be like Freddie, and get serious about sun protection!

FREDDIE FREEMAN FUN FACTS

- In 2014, during a rare snowstorm in usually sunny and hot Atlanta, Freeman got stuck in traffic for hours. His former teammate Chipper Jones rescued him on an ATV. The event was so memorable that it was commemorated with a bobblehead (Sandler, 2020).
- In 2020, Freddie got COVID-19 and was really sick. He thought he might not make it, but he made an amazing recovery and went on to win the NL MVP award later that season (Sandler, 2020).

THINGS TO THINK ABOUT

- Freddie ensures that he's protected from the dangers of sunlight. What are some ways you can stay safe when playing sports?
- Freddie established himself in more than one position on the field. Which roles would you like to play on the baseball diamond?

UP NEXT

Now that we've explored Freddie Freeman's inspiring journey, let's move on to another great player: Juan Soto.

Juan's rise to Major League Baseball fame was hard-earned through his extraordinary talent, strong work ethic, and deep passion for the game. Born in the Dominican Republic, Soto quickly made a name for himself with his powerful swing and keen eye at the plate. His path, from a promising young prospect to a World Series champion and one of the most feared hitters today, is filled with notable achievements and memorable moments just waiting for us to discover.

NE
Nationals

Chapter 5

JUAN SOTO

It don't matter what is going on. It don't matter what is happening, never stop. Just keep going.

–JUAN SOTO

Juan Soto's baseball success story, from playing in local leagues to becoming one of the youngest and most promising stars in MLB, is one of rapid ascent and continuous skill development.

His rise to stardom has been meteoric. Signed by the Washington Nationals as an international free agent at just 16, three years later, he was already making headlines in the majors, displaying a maturity and confidence at the plate that belied his years. Let's learn his story of triumph and great ball playing.

JUAN'S STORY

Juan Soto's journey from the rough streets of Santo Domingo, Dominican Republic to the bright lights of Major League Baseball is a tale of determination and strong support from his family.

Juan's passion for baseball was clear from a young age, encouraged by his dad, Juan Soto Sr., who played as a catcher in a local men's league. Growing up in a tough neighborhood, Juan's mom limited his outdoor time, leading him to get creative with his baseball practice. He fashioned makeshift balls from crumpled paper and tape, even playing baseball inside the house when his mom said it was too dangerous to go outside.

Naturally right-handed, Juan took his dad's advice to bat and throw left-handed, something that would give him a strategic edge in the sport. There's nothing that pitchers hate more than a left-handed batter.

In 2015, Juan kicked off his professional baseball career by signing with the Washington Nationals. He was only 16 years old at the time. Signing onto the Nationals' organization as an international free agent, he received a whopping $1.5 million signing bonus, showing the high expectations the team placed on his potential (*Juan Soto*, 2024b).

Juan's tour through the Nationals' minor league teams was stellar, even though he faced some injuries that limited his game time. He made his minor leagues debut in 2016 with the Gulf Coast League Nationals and was named the MVP that season after hitting .368 with five home runs and 32 RBIs (*Juan Soto*, 2024b).

Even though he suffered a fractured ankle and a wrist injury that required surgery on his left hand, Juan quickly progressed through the minors, hitting .373 with five home runs and 24 RBIs in just 16 games with the Hagerstown Suns before being promoted to the Potomac Nationals and then the Harrisburg Senators (*Juan Soto*, 2024b).

Juan made his eagerly anticipated MLB debut with the Washington Nationals on May 20, 2018, at the age of 19, making him the youngest player in the major leagues at that time. His impact was immediate. In his first start, he hit a whopping 422-foot home run on the first pitch of his first at-bat, stunning the crowd (*Juan Soto*, 2024b).

Juan finished his rookie season with 22 home runs and 70 RBIs, almost getting named Rookie of the Year (*Juan Soto*, 2024a). His rookie season was marked by intense discipline at the plate, finishing with a .292 batting average and a .406 on-base percentage. He set several MLB records for his age group, including the most multiple home run games by a teenage player (*Juan Soto*, 2024b).

The 2019 season saw Juan elevate his game even further. He played an important part in the Nationals' path to their first World Series title. Juan's postseason performance was amazing, as he got crucial home runs and game-changing plays.

In the World Series, Juan batted .333 with three home runs and seven RBIs, earning co-recipient honors of the Babe Ruth Award for his outstanding postseason performance (*Juan Soto*, 2024b). His contributions were vital to the Nationals' championship run, confirming his position as one of the league's brightest young stars.

Over the next few years, Juan continued to improve and establish himself as one of the most feared home run sluggers. In the 2020 season, which was shortened due to the COVID-19 pandemic, he led the National League with a .351 batting average and a .490 on-base percentage, showing exceptional hitting ability and plate discipline (*Juan Soto*, 2024b). His ability to consistently get on base and hit for power made him a cornerstone of the Nationals' lineup. Soto's remarkable 2021 season saw him lead the league in walks and on-base percentage, reinforcing his status as one of the game's most disciplined hitters.

In December 2023, Juan got traded to the New York Yankees in a blockbuster deal. Joining a star-studded lineup, he brought his exceptional skills to the Bronx Bombers and became a sensation.

Juan has had a tremendous start to the 2024 season, leading the Yankees in several offensive categories, including batting average and home runs. Known for his ability to perform under intense pressure, he's been delivering game-winning hits, including a dramatic go-ahead home run against the Astros on Opening Day.

Juan's reputation for performing in high-pressure situations has continued throughout the season. His ability to stay calm and deliver when it matters most has made him a fan favorite and a feared opponent.

In 2024, Soto set a new record for the highest arbitration salary, agreeing to a one-year, $31 million deal with the Yankees (Langs, 2024). This deal surpassed the previous record held by Shohei Ohtani, highlighting Soto's value and impact in the league. Thanks to his outstanding performance on the field, at the time of the writing of this book, Juan is currently a leading contender for the American League MVP award.

His ability to continue playing at such a high level has made him one of the top players in the league. His rise in Major League Baseball continues to inspire young athletes around the world, demonstrating that with determination and skill, anything is possible.

JUAN SOTO FUN FACTS

- Juan has his own pre-game rituals, and one of them is eating delicious Dominican food that reminds him of home. His favorite dish is *pastelón de plátano maduro*, a kind of lasagna-type dish made with sweet plantains and rib meat. His mom makes the best version of it!
- Juan is known for his signature dance move: the "Soto Shuffle." Done to intimidate opposing players, he swings his hips and traces his foot through the dirt in the batter's box.

THINGS TO THINK ABOUT

- Imagine you hit a game-winning homer in front of thousands of fans. How would you celebrate with your teammates?
- If you had a unique dance like the "Soto Shuffle," what would it be, and why?

UP NEXT

Now that we've learned about Juan Soto's path to baseball fame, let's turn our attention to another dynamic and influential player who has left an indelible mark on Major League Baseball: Bryce Harper.

Bryce's career has been a testament to raw talent, relentless determination, and a deep love for the game. From his prodigious beginnings as a teenage phenom to his current status as a seasoned veteran and leader, Bryce's story is one of overcoming challenges, achieving milestones, and consistently playing as hard as he can. Let's meet another player who has captivated fans and critics alike with his extraordinary skills and deep passion for the game!

Phillies
Harper

Chapter 6

BRYCE HARPER

I'd rather be a good person off the field than a good baseball player on the field.

–BRYCE HARPER

Bryce Harper, as he suggests in the quote that opens this chapter, is known for more than his accomplishments as an athlete; he's a person who values character and integrity above all else. From his early years as a baseball prodigy in Las Vegas to his standout performances in MLB, Bryce has always shown his passion for the game and has shown his generous nature off the field too.

Bryce's story is one of talent, grit, and character. His story serves as an inspiration, not just for aspiring athletes like you, but to anyone who wants to pursue the things they care about while maintaining integrity and humility. As we start to learn about the details of Harper's career, we'll uncover the layers of dedication and passion that have come to define this remarkable athlete. Let's learn Bryce's story.

BRYCE'S STORY

Bryce's story begins in Las Vegas, Nevada, where he was born. From the time he was a little kid, he showed an exceptional amount of talent in baseball. As he continued to mature and started taking baseball more seriously, it quickly became his passion and life focus.

His early years were marked by an intense dedication to improving his skills, often practicing with his father, Ron, who worked long hours as an ironworker. Bryce attended Las Vegas High School, where his talents on the field became clear to all who saw him play, even attracting national attention. By the time he was 16, he had already been featured on the cover of *Sports Illustrated*, the headline proclaiming that he was the "Chosen One"!

Bryce made the bold decision to leave high school early, deciding to get his GED instead of a high school degree to speed up his eligibility for the MLB draft. But skipping his high school graduation ceremony didn't mean he wasn't serious about education; far from it! In fact, Bryce getting his GED allowed him to enroll at the College of Southern Nevada, a school that's known for having a great baseball team: the Coyotes.

Even though he was just 17 at the time, Bryce dominated the field with the Coyotes, hitting .443 with 31 home runs and 98 RBIs in 66 games (*Bryce Harper*, 2024). His performance earned him the 2010 SWAC Player of the Year award and the Golden Spikes Award, the national award for the best amateur baseball player.

In 2010, the Washington Nationals selected Bryce as the first overall draft pick, recognizing his strong potential. Bryce made his MLB debut in 2012 when he was 19, and he quickly made an impact on the field with his skills and competitive spirit. In his debut season, he won the NL Rookie of the Year award, boasting a .270 batting average, 22 home runs, and 59 RBIs (*Bryce Harper*, 2024). He was also invited to play in the All-Star Game, the youngest position player to ever receive this honor.

Bryce's breakout season came in 2015 when he had what ended up being one the best offensive seasons of any player in recent memory.

At just 22 years old, he won the NL MVP award, becoming the youngest player to receive the award with a unanimous vote. That season, Bryce led the league in home runs, on-base percentage, and slugging percentage (*Bryce Harper*, 2024).

In 2019, Bryce entered free agency and signed an epic $330 million contract with the Philadelphia Phillies for an impressive 13 years, one of the largest and longest-duration contracts in sports history at the time (Wells, n.d.). This move marked a new chapter in his career, bringing his talents to a team eager to return to relevance in MLB.

Then, disaster struck. Like Shohei Ohtani, he needed Tommy John surgery for a torn ligament. Remarkably, Bryce made a swift recovery in 2023. To ease the strain on his arm, he temporarily switched to playing first base.

His strength on the field paid off, and by 2024, Bryce was put in as the starting first baseman for the National League in the All-Star Game. Additionally, he was honored as the NL Player of the Month for May for his continued excellence on the field.

Bryce's performance in the 2024 season so far has been filled with memorable moments, including a standout performance in the London Series against the Mets, where he celebrated a home run with a soccer-style slide, sending fans and teammates into a frenzy. This wasn't a show-offy move but a sign of pure joy and his deep love for the game.

Throughout his career, Bryce has faced other injuries besides the torn ligament, but he's consistently shown the ability to recover and return to peak performance. His determination and passion for baseball have been evident in every comeback, inspiring fans and fellow players alike.

Off the field, Bryce has been involved in charitable activities, supporting various causes and giving back to the community. Bryce is a married man, and he and his wife Kayla have three kids together. Bryce has said that he developed a strong work ethic from all the lessons he learned from his dad as a kid. He has never forgotten the importance of hard work to achieve big payoffs.

Bryce's religious background is also an important part of his life. He's a member of the Church of Jesus Christ of Latter-Day Saints. Bryce has spoken about the influence of his faith on his life and career, mentioning that he strives to be a positive example both on and off the field.

Bryce's baseball story is one of faith, strength, and character. His story serves as an inspiration, not just for aspiring young athletes like you, but to anyone who wants to achieve big things and have a big heart too.

BRYCE HARPER FUN FACTS

- Bryce is known for his unique batting stance called the "Harper Hunch," where he leans forward with his back knee almost touching the ground!
- Bryce has a custom bat model called the Harper 3, made by Louisville Slugger.
- He won the Home Run Derby in 2018 at Nationals Park in Washington, D.C., thrilling the crowd with his awesome power-hitting. That same year, *Time* magazine named Harper one of the 100 Most Influential People in the world!
- Bryce has supported different charitable causes, including the Leukemia & Lymphoma Society and the Make-A-Wish Foundation.

- Growing up in Las Vegas, he still roots for his hometown teams, including the Golden Knights hockey team.
- Bryce has gained a dedicated fan following known as "Harper's Heroes," who passionately cheer him on during games.

THINGS TO THINK ABOUT

- If you created your own unique batting stance like Bryce did, what would you call it, and why?
- How would you stay motivated and positive if you had to recover from a major injury and surgery like Bryce did?
- Who is your sports hero, and what qualities do you admire most about them?

UP NEXT

After following the inspiring journey of Bryce Harper, from his Las Vegas upbringing to his star-studded presence in baseball today, let's now turn our attention to another remarkable talent: Clayton Kershaw.

Known for his dominant pitching and leadership on the mound, Clayton has become a key player in MLB today.

LA
Dodgers
22
LA

Chapter 7

CLAYTON KERSHAW

I firmly believe that you are supposed to love everybody. That is God's one boldest commandment.

–CLAYTON KERSHAW

The words from Clayton Kershaw that open this chapter reflect not just his approach to life but also the positive attitude he shows on the field. His path to baseball fame, from a promising young pitcher in Texas to one of the most dominant forces in MLB, shows his talent, hard work, and die-hard commitment to his principles.

Known for his skills on the mound and his dedication to generosity off the field, Kershaw's story is one of exquisite baseball skills, combined with the power of faith. In this chapter, we'll follow his rise to stardom, look at the challenges he has overcome, and learn about the lasting impact he continues to make, both in baseball and beyond.

CLAYTON'S STORY

Clayton Kershaw was born in Dallas, Texas. From the time he was just a boy, it was clear that he had a great talent for baseball. Raised by his mom after his parents got divorced when he was 10, Clayton found purpose on the baseball diamond.

Clayton's early years were spent playing in local youth leagues, where his natural ability and competitive spirit quickly drew attention. By the time he started high school, he was already a standout athlete. His senior year was especially remarkable, as he posted a perfect 13-0 record with an astonishing 0.77 ERA, striking out 139 batters in just 64 innings (*Clayton Kershaw*, 2024). One of his most memorable high school performances was the all-strikeout perfect game he pitched, where he struck out 15 batters, and then to top it all off, hit a grand slam!

Recognizing his immense potential, the Los Angeles Dodgers decided to draft him. Clayton was the seventh overall pick in the 2006 MLB Draft. At the time, he was considered the top high school pitcher available, and he did not disappoint. Kershaw quickly ascended through various minor league teams thanks to his powerful fastball, devastating curveball, and commendable work ethic.

By 2008, just two years after being drafted, Kershaw finally made his MLB debut with the Dodgers at the age of 20, becoming the youngest player in the league at that time. His rookie season was a solid foundation for what would come to be a legendary career, marked by his ability to strike out batters and his calm composure on the mound.

Clayton's breakout season came in 2011. He led the National League in wins with 21, boasting an ERA of 2.28 with 248 strikeouts, giving him a rare pitching Triple Crown (*Clayton Kershaw*, 2024). He was awarded his first Cy Young Award, the prestigious honor given to the best pitcher in the entire league.

Clayton's success continued over the next several years. He won the Cy Young Award again in 2013 and 2014, making him a rare three-time recipient! His 2014 season was particularly noteworthy. That year, Clayton won not just the Cy Young, but was also named the NL MVP. He was the first pitcher to win the MVP since Bob Gibson in 1968. That year, he finished the season with a 21-3 record with a 1.77 ERA (*Clayton Kershaw*, 2024).

On June 18, 2014, Clayton threw a no-hitter against the Colorado Rockies, striking out 15 batters without allowing a single walk. The only blemish on his record that night was an error by his teammate, Hanley Ramirez, which prevented Clayton from achieving a perfect game. Despite this, his performance was widely regarded as one of the best pitching displays in baseball history, showing his incredible control and skill on the mound.

Despite all his successes, Clayton's career has been interrupted by injuries. He has faced setbacks during training and the regular season, including back and shoulder issues, that have forced him to spend time on the injured list. Each time, however, Clayton has worked diligently to return to top form. His amazing ability to bounce back from injuries and continue performing shows just how dedicated he is to the game.

In the 2023 season, Clayton proved that he still had plenty of gas left in the tank. Despite dealing with injuries, he finished the season with a 2.46 ERA, having struck out 137 batters over 131.2 innings (*Clayton Kershaw*, 2024). His performance again showed his continued skill and effectiveness on the mound, even as he carefully managed his growing physical health challenges.

After undergoing shoulder surgery in late 2023, Clayton faced a long recovery process. Determined to return to the game he loves, he dedicated himself to his rehab program with the same intensity he brings to the mound.

At the time of this book's writing, Clayton is making steady progress, participating in rehab assignments and gradually working his way back to full strength. His commitment to his own recovery is evident as he takes each step methodically, ensuring he can continue to contribute to the Dodgers.

In a promising sign of his recovery, Clayton began a rehab assignment with the Single-A Rancho Cucamonga Quakes, pitching three innings and striking out five batters. His successful outing showed that he was on track to rejoin the Dodgers' rotation soon. This return marked a big milestone in his journey back from injury and showed the level of determination he had.

Off the field, Clayton is known for his charity work. He and his wife, Ellen, founded an organization called Kershaw's Challenge, which supports various causes globally. His humanitarian work, including donating $100 per strikeout and supporting other charitable initiatives, has shown his dedication to making a positive impact on the world.

One of his most well-known projects was the construction of an orphanage in Zambia called Hope's Home. Inspired by an 11-year-old girl named Hope who is HIV-positive, the orphanage provides a safe haven for children in need.

Looking ahead, Clayton remains determined to return to full strength and help the Dodgers in their pursuit of another World Series title. His dedication to the game and his team is unwavering, and baseball fans nationwide eagerly await his continued success on the mound.

CLAYTON KERSHAW FUN FACTS

- Clayton's notorious curveball is one of the most devastating pitches in modern baseball.

- Clayton is the great-nephew of Clyde Tombaugh, the astronomer who discovered the dwarf planet Pluto!
- A devout Methodist Christian, Clayton has shared his faith journey online and in books he's published along with his wife. His commitment to his faith and family gives him strength and perspective both on and off the field.

THINGS TO THINK ABOUT

- If you could develop one amazing sports skill like Clayton's curveball, what would it be, and why?
- If you were the captain of a sports team, how would you encourage and support your teammates during tough times?

UP NEXT

Clayton Kershaw's path to baseball fame has been nothing short of inspiring, marked by exceptional talent, dedication, and resilience. From his early days in Dallas, to his numerous records and awards, he has left a strong impression on the sport.

Now let's turn our attention to another extraordinary pitcher who's made a big impact on the game: Max Scherzer. Scherzer's career, characterized by his fierce competitiveness and awesome achievements, offers yet another compelling narrative in the major leagues.

W
Nationals

Chapter 8

MAX SCHERZER

Any time I've put extra work in, I see results.

–MAX SCHERZER

Known for his intensity on the field, Max Scherzer has a reputation for being one of MLB's greatest pitchers. From growing up a young baseball enthusiast in Chesterfield, Missouri, to becoming a multi-time Cy Young Award winner, Max's story is one of dedication and a continued commitment to the sport.

As we learn Max's story, we'll look at his early life, his rise through the ranks of professional baseball, and the key moments that have helped him blaze his career. From his modest beginnings back home in Missouri, to his stints with multiple MLB teams, Max's journey is filled with many moments of both glory and struggle. Let's learn Max's story.

MAX'S STORY

Born in Chesterfield, Missouri, Max was in love with baseball from a young age. As a kid growing up in the St. Louis suburb, he naturally idolized the Cardinals. Watching his favorite team play as often as he could, after school, he'd go and practice his skills on the local baseball diamonds.

His dedication to the sport was clear as soon as he got to high school, where he played baseball, and also football and basketball, allowing him to flex his full range of athletic skills. His intense competitive nature set him apart from other kids early on.

Max's talents in high school sports earned him a place at the University of Missouri, where he continued to impress. Known for his power and seriousness on the mound, during college, he refined his skills and grew into the great pitcher he is today.

One of Max's college coaches helped him learn how to pitch with more balance and control, and this improved his performance significantly. Playing in the Big 12, he was named Pitcher of the Year in 2005. Later, he was inducted into the University of Missouri Intercollegiate Athletics Hall of Fame.

In 2006, Max was drafted by the Arizona Diamondbacks, making him Missouri's first-ever MLB first-round draft pick. He made his debut with the Diamondbacks in 2008, and his dogged determination quickly became his trademark. His performance caught the attention of the Detroit Tigers, who acquired him in a trade in 2009.

While Max's playing with the Diamondbacks was great, his time with the Tigers was simply transformative. Teaming up with Justin Verlander, Max became a key player in the rotation. He managed to make some big strides in his career, highlighted by winning his first Cy Young Award in 2013. That season, he posted a remarkable 21-3 record with a 2.90 ERA and 240 strikeouts, confirming his status as one of the league's top pitchers (Adler, 2022). His efforts led to four consecutive AL Central title wins from 2011 to 2014, and a 2012 World Series appearance.

Max's career took a turn in 2015 when he signed a $210 million, seven-year contract to play with the Washington Nationals (*Max*

Scherzer, 2024). There, he won two more Cy Young Awards, in 2016 and 2017, and played an important part in leading the Nationals to their first World Series title in 2019.

Max's dominance on the mound, combined with his determination to win, made him a key part of the Nationals' success. He became only the sixth pitcher in MLB history to win the Cy Young Award in both the AL and NL (*Max Scherzer*, 2024).

In 2021, Max was traded to the Los Angeles Dodgers, where he continued to display his exceptional skills. His time with the Dodgers was marked by outstanding performances. He posted a 1.98 ERA with the Dodgers and helped lead them to the NLCS, finishing third in the Cy Young voting for that year (*Max Scherzer*, 2024). The following year, he signed a record-breaking $130 million contract with the New York Mets for three years (*Max Scherzer*, 2024).

By 2023, Max had found a new home with the Texas Rangers due to a mid-season trade. Despite facing a big setback when he needed surgery for a herniated disk, his comeback for the 2024 season was inspiring. In his debut for the Rangers, he pitched five scoreless innings, showing everyone his undiminished skill. His performance in the 2024 season demonstrated that even after multiple surgeries, and now, at the age of 39, he remains a force to reckon with on the mound.

Off the field, Max is known for his strong family values and his advocacy for various social causes. He is married to Erica May, a former pitcher for the Mizzou softball team, and together they have four children. The Scherzers are actively involved in charity efforts, including raising awareness and funds to combat human trafficking through their initiative, Strike Out Modern Slavery. They are also dedicated to animal welfare, supporting the Humane Rescue Alliance and covering adoption fees for rescue animals.

Their commitment to giving back is as strong as Max's dedication to his sport.

Max is very close with his family. His brother, Alex, who tragically passed away, had always been a big source of motivation throughout his career. Alex loved baseball too, and he had a deep influence on Max because he helped him understand and appreciate sabermetrics. Sabermetrics is a fancy word for a special type of baseball math. It helps players, coaches, and fans understand the game better by using numbers and statistics. Instead of just looking at a player's batting average or home runs, sabermetrics looks at many different numbers to figure out how good a player really is.

Max dedicates every start to his late brother's memory. This personal loss has fueled his drive and passion for the game, pushing him to continually be the best he can to honor his brother's memory.

MAX SCHERZER FUN FACTS

- Max Scherzer has a unique optical condition called heterochromia iridium, which gave him two different colored eyes! One is blue, and the other is brown!
- He's sometimes known as "Mad Max," due to his intense and competitive nature on the mound and the way he intimidates batters.
- He has over 3,000 strikeouts, and has achieved three so-called "immaculate innings." This is when a pitcher strikes out all three batters in an inning with just nine pitches.

THINGS TO THINK ABOUT

- If you could throw a fastball like Max, how fast would you want it to be, and what would you name your special pitch?

- If you had heterochromia, which two eye colors do you think would be cool? Name any color you choose! It doesn't have to be a real human or animal eye color. Use your imagination!
- If you were a star athlete, what fun activities would you do with your fans to show your appreciation?

UP NEXT

After learning about "Mad Max" Scherzer, a pitcher known for the fear and intimidation he strikes into batters, as he strikes them out one after the other, it's time to shift our focus to another extraordinary player. Enter Pete Alonso, a world-class slugger whose impact on the game is as powerful as his swings.

From Pete's early days in the minor leagues to his record-breaking performances in Major League Baseball, his story is one about raw talent and the ability to shine under pressure. Let's explore the story of Pete Alonso, a player who has carved out a significant place in the annals of baseball history with his incredible power and top-notch performance.

Mets

Chapter 9

PETE ALONSO

Believe in us. And don't just believe. Know. ... Just smile, and know that we've got this.

–PETE ALONSO

From his early days in Tampa, Florida, to becoming one of the most impressive power hitters in Major League Baseball, Pete's path to major league success is a story of dedication and passion for the game.

In this chapter, we'll explore the life and career of the player affectionately known as "Polar Bear," looking at the milestones that have shaped his path to stardom and the qualities that make him an exceptional athlete and leader.

Through triumphs and challenges, and always while maintaining a steadfast commitment to his team, Pete's story is one of inspiration and sports excellence. Let's learn the life story of this awesome player, from his beginnings to his current status as a powerhouse in the world of baseball!

PETE'S STORY

Pete was born in Tampa, Florida. When it was time for him to start high school, he first went to a private Jesuit high school for his freshman and sophomore years, but later transferred to public school. He used to play all different sports, including lacrosse and football, but eventually, he decided to focus more on baseball, where he showed talent as a third baseman. This decision set the stage for his future success.

Pete's abilities in high school earned him a spot on the Gators at the University of Florida, where he switched to first base. His college career was the stuff legends are made of. In his freshman year, he was named to the All-Star team in his school's division. By his junior year, he boasted an impressive .374 with 14 home runs and 60 RBIs (*Pete Alonso*, 2024).

He continued to play great baseball, opting to play in the collegiate summer league for teams in Wisconsin and Massachusetts rather than taking a break from sports during summer vacation. During his junior year with the Gators, he hit .374 with 14 home runs and 60 RBIs, leading the team to the College World Series in both 2015 and 2016 (*Pete Alonso*, 2024). His performance in college made him widely recognized as one of the top prospects in the country.

In the 2016 MLB Draft, Pete's dreams of becoming a professional baseball player came true. He was drafted by the New York Mets. His first stop in the Mets organization was playing with the Brooklyn Cyclones. Pete quickly made a name for himself in the minor leagues. He batted five home runs in just 30 games that season, finishing with an impressive .322 batting average (*Pete Alonso*, 2024). He also earned a spot on the league's All-Star team.

Pete's rapid ascent through the minor leagues continued in 2017 and 2018. He played with the St. Lucie Mets and went on to play with the Binghamton Rumble Ponies, and finally, with the Las Vegas 51s. His impressive stats, including a .285 batting average,

36 home runs, and 119 RBIs in 2018, earned him the Joe Bauman Home Run Award (*Pete Alonso*, 2024). By the end of the 2018 season, Pete was ranked as one of the Mets' top prospects, ready to make his mark in the majors.

Pete's major league debut came on Opening Day in 2019, and he wasted no time making an impact. He got his first major league hit against the Nationals and hit his first home run just days later. His rookie season was shaping up to be one for the record books. He ended up setting a new MLB rookie record with 53 home runs, surpassing Aaron Judge's previous mark (*Pete Alonso*, 2024). His performance earned him the NL Rookie of the Year and a spot on the All-MLB First Team. Pete's power at the plate and charismatic personality quickly made him a fan favorite.

Pete's excellent playing wasn't only limited to the regular season. He showed off his power in the Home Run Derby, winning the event in 2019, and again in 2021. These victories further confirmed his reputation for being one of the league's premier sluggers. Over the next few seasons, Pete remained one of the top power hitters in the league.

In March 2022, Pete survived a terrifying car accident, which he described as a "really close experience to death" (*Pete Alonso*, 2024). This incident renewed his appreciation for life and his drive to make a positive impact both on and off the field. In 2023, he bounced back from his brush with death, hitting 40 home runs and driving in 120 runs (*Pete Alonso*, 2024).

As Pete headed into the 2024 season, the Mets agreed to a $20.5 million one-year contract extension (*Pete Alonso*, 2024). This deal set the stage for Pete's upcoming free agency, sparking speculation about his future with the team. Despite facing challenges, such as a hand injury early in the 2024 season, Pete's strength was on full display as he quickly recovered and returned to the lineup.

Off the field, Pete's personal life is as inspiring as his professional career. He formed The Alonso Foundation in 2020 with his wife Haley to support youth, veteran, and animal causes. Pete's commitment to giving back to the community is deeply revealing of his character and values.

As Pete looks to the seasons ahead, his goal remains clear: to help the Mets compete for a championship and secure a long-term contract that reflects his value to the team and the sport he loves playing.

PETE ALONSO FUN FACTS

- Pete is affectionately known as "Polar Bear," a nickname given to him by his college coach because of his immense strength and power.
- Pete has proven his power in the MLB Home Run Derby, winning the title twice. His impressive performances have made him a fan favorite in this exciting event.
- He enjoys hunting and fishing, activities that allow him to unwind and connect with nature.

THINGS TO THINK ABOUT

- If you could participate in a Home Run Derby, what song would you choose as the music they play as you step up to the plate, and why?
- If you had a fun animal-inspired nickname like "Polar Bear," what would it be and what would it represent about you?

UP NEXT

Now that we've learned about Pete Alonso's journey and his impact on baseball, it's time to move on to another remarkable player: José Altuve!

José's story is one of talent and dedication, making him a standout figure in baseball. His impressive career and contributions to the sport continue to inspire fans and fellow players alike. Let's learn about his life and how he made it to the top of the game.

ASTROS
27

Chapter 10

JOSÉ ALTUVE

In baseball, it doesn't matter if you're tall, skinny, fat, whatever. If you really have talent and you really love to play, I feel like you can make it.

–JOSÉ ALTUVE

José Altuve's story is one of athletic performance that packs a punch, showing us that great baseball skills can come in small packages. Standing at just 5 feet 6 inches. José defied the odds and silenced the critics who doubted his potential due to his height.

His path to baseball excellence, from the streets of Maracay, Venezuela, to becoming one of Major League Baseball's most revered players, is highly inspiring. Altuve's career with the Houston Astros is a tale of talent, hard work, and passion for the game. This chapter is all about José's climb to the top of professional baseball. We'll learn about his early struggles, his rise to stardom, and the unbeatable spirit that has made him a beloved figure in baseball.

JOSÉ'S STORY

José Altuve was born in Maracay, Venezuela. From the time he was very young, he was totally obsessed with baseball! His passion for the game only grew stronger as he practiced and played more.

Despite his undeniable talent, his small size caused many to doubt his potential. Once he was fully grown, he still only stood at 5' 6", but he was determined to pursue a professional career in the sport.

Scouts and coaches often dismissed José. They thought that his height would put him at a major disadvantage. However, José's unwavering determination and love for the game kept him pushing forward. He was going to prove his doubters wrong.

In 2007, when he was just 16, Altuve had the chance of a lifetime. He was invited to a tryout camp held by the Houston Astros right in his hometown. At first, the scouts weren't sure about his capabilities. They thought he was a bit too young, and small. They didn't even believe that he was 16, as he still looked like a child, so they had to turn him away.

José went home that day, but he refused to give up. He returned to the tryout camp the next day with his birth certificate in hand, ready to prove himself. His persistence paid off—after showing off his skills and proving everyone wrong, he was signed by the Astros as an amateur free agent, marking the beginning of his professional baseball career!

José's minor league career was marked by impressive performances that quickly propelled him through the ranks. He began in the Venezuelan Summer League, where he hit .343, before moving to the United States to play for the Greeneville Astros (*José Altuve*, 2024).

His talent on the field with the Astros was undeniable, hitting .324 with 21 stolen bases in just 45 games in 2009 (*José Altuve*, 2024). By 2011, he was dominating the minor leagues, posting a .389 average with 24 steals across various tiers of the Astros' minor league system (*José Altuve*, 2024). His performance earned him the Astros Minor League Player of the Year award and a long-awaited mid-season call-up to the majors. Finally, he had accomplished his dream.

José made his MLB debut with the Houston Astros on July 20, 2011. He quickly became a fixture in the lineup, showing off his great batting and defensive skills. Over the next few years, José firmed up his reputation as one of the best second basemen in the game. He earned his first All-Star selection in 2012 and has been selected nine times throughout his career to date.

One of José's most notable achievements came in 2017 when he won the AL MVP award. That year, he led the Astros to their first World Series championship, batting an impressive .346 with 24 home runs and 32 stolen bases (*José Altuve*, 2024). José's performance in the postseason was instrumental in the Astros' success, and his leadership both on and off the field made him a beloved figure in Houston.

José's impact on the Astros continued beyond 2017. In 2019, he hit a jaw-dropping walk-off home run, clinching the AL Championship Series win. In 2022, he played a key part in the team's World Series victory, further confirming his legacy as one of the greatest players in franchise history. In February 2024, José signed a $125 million contract extension with the Astros, ensuring he would remain with the team through the 2029 season (Footer, 2024).

Throughout his career, Altuve has faced and overcome many challenges. Having to deal with injuries, including a thumb fracture in 2023, he achieved quick recoveries and returned to top form each time. Looking ahead to the 2024 season, Altuve is healthy, motivated, and committed to helping the Astros compete for another championship.

Off the field, Altuve's personal life reflects his grounded nature. He married his longtime girlfriend, Nina, in 2016, and the couple welcomed their first child later that year. Altuve is also a born-again Christian and frequently speaks about his faith and its importance in his life. Despite his success, he has faced some scary moments, including a burglary at his home in March 2023, where over $1 million in jewelry was stolen (*José Altuve*, 2024).

Through all the highs and lows, José's love for baseball and his unwavering determination have remained constant. His journey from an overlooked player in Venezuela to a key figure in Major League Baseball is a testament to sheer will. His story of being called too short yet making it to the top continues to inspire fans and aspiring young athletes like you, proving that no obstacle is too great with enough passion and dedication.

JOSÉ ALTUVE FUN FACTS

- José has won six Silver Slugger awards.
- Fans created a fun way to measure distances the ball travels in units of measurement called "Altuves," with one Altuve being equivalent to 5' 5," even though his height is frequently listed as 5' 6".
- Fellow Venezuelan MLB player, Víctor Martínez, has been a mentor to José, helping him navigate the ups and downs of professional baseball.

THINGS TO THINK ABOUT

- If you were told you were too small or not good enough for something you love, how would you prove everyone wrong?
- If you could meet any baseball player, past or present, who would it be and what would you ask them?

UP NEXT

After learning about the inspiring journey of José Altuve and witnessing his incredible impact on the game of baseball, it's time to shift our focus to another extraordinary player who has made his mark in the sport.

Our next chapter peering into the stories of today's baseball greats brings us to Justin Verlander, a name synonymous with pitching excellence. Justin has had a career filled with some incredible achievements and unforgettable moments. Let's jump right into the story of this legendary pitcher and explore how his dedication and skill have shaped his career and left a big impression on the world of baseball.

Detroit
35

Chapter 11

JUSTIN VERLANDER

All I know is that if I continue to pitch well, good things will keep happening.

–JUSTIN VERLANDER

From his early days growing up in Virginia to his dominance on the mound in Major League Baseball, Justin's baseball success story is one worth knowing. As one of the top pitchers of his generation, Verlander's career has been marked by milestones that continue to reveal his shining talent on the field.

In this chapter, we'll explore Justin's life and career, looking at some of the key moments that have shaped his path and the lessons we can learn from his amazing story. Let's do it! Let's learn Justin's Story.

JUSTIN'S STORY

Justin Verlander was born in Manakin-Sabot, Virginia. From a young age, his passion for baseball was strong. Once his dad saw him swing a bat for the first time, he immediately recognized Justin's potential and decided to enroll him in the Richmond Baseball Academy, where Justin's skills began to flourish. His fastball, which quickly reached speeds of 84 mph, set him apart from his peers (*Justin Verlander*, 2022).

Justin's talent earned him a spot on the team at Old Dominion University, where he continued to make waves. With the Old Dominion Monarchs, he set a bunch of records, including the school's career strikeout record, with 427 (*Justin Verlander*, 2022). His impressive playing caught the attention of major league scouts, setting the stage for what would come to be an amazing professional career.

In the 2004 MLB Draft, the Detroit Tigers selected Justin as the second overall pick. He quickly rose through the minor league ranks, making his MLB debut the next year, on the Fourth of July. Although his initial outings were challenging, Justin's potential was undeniable.

His breakout came in 2006 when he helped the Tigers reach the World Series. His stellar performance earned him the American League Rookie of the Year award. Justin finished the season with a 17-9 record and a 3.63 ERA, making him widely recognized as a top-tier pitcher (*Justin Verlander*, 2022).

Justin's dominance on the mound was further confirmed by his pitching three different no-hitters. His first one was against the Milwaukee Brewers in the summer of 2007. He followed this with a second no-hitter four years later against the Toronto Blue Jays, and a third in 2019, against the Blue Jays. These feats showed his rare levels of control and power on the mound.

The peak of Justin's career came in 2011 when he won both the Cy Young and MVP awards in the American League. His season was amazing, as he led the league in wins, strikeouts, and ERA, earning him the prestigious pitching Triple Crown.

Justin's career took a new turn when he was traded to the Houston Astros in 2017. His arrival was a game-changer, and he led the Astros to their first World Series championship. He was named the

ALCS MVP for his efforts. In 2022, he helped the Astros secure another World Series title, further cementing his legacy in the sport.

Despite enduring serious injuries, including Tommy John surgery in 2020 (a procedure to repair a torn ligament in the arm), Justin's resilience has been inspiring. He missed the entire 2021 season but made a triumphant return in 2022, winning 18 games and earning his third Cy Young Award with a sub-2.00 ERA (*Justin Verlander*, 2022).

After a mid-season trade back to the Astros in 2023, Justin played a key role in their rotation, showing that he could adapt and excel even after injuries. The 2024 season saw Justin starting on the injured list due to a shoulder issue. However, he made a successful debut in April, pitching six strong innings with four strikeouts, showing that he could still perform at a high level.

Justin continues to reach new milestones, including surpassing 3,000 career strikeouts and 250 career wins (*Justin Verlander*, 2022). These achievements prove his longevity and consistency in the game. Looking ahead, Justin aims to stay healthy and contribute to another championship run for the Astros. He's also focused on mentoring the next generation of pitchers, passing on his wealth of knowledge and experience.

Justin's life off the field is equally inspiring. His journey and development are detailed in a book his parents wrote about what it's like to be parents to a baseball star called: *Rocks Across the Pond: Lessons Learned, Stories Told.*

In 2016, Justin founded the Wins For Warriors Foundation to help support military veterans. His dedication to this cause had already earned him the Bob Feller Act of Valor Award a few years earlier.

Justin's story is one of exceptional talent, mental focus, and exquisite baseball skills. As he continues to defy the odds and reach new heights, he remains a true inspiration to young baseball players, both on and off the field.

JUSTIN VERLANDER FUN FACTS

- Throughout his career, Justin has acted as a mentor to younger players, sharing his knowledge and experience to help others grow.
- Among fans and teammates, Verlander is affectionately known as "JV."
- Justin is married to the supermodel Kate Upton. The couple tied the knot in 2017 and have a daughter together.
- Justin has made some successful endorsement deals, partnering with major brands like Nike and Chevrolet.

THINGS TO THINK ABOUT

- Is there someone in your life who inspires you to overcome challenges, just like Verlander overcame his injuries?
- Imagine you could achieve one major milestone in your favorite sport. What would it be, and why?

UP NEXT

After learning about Justin Verlander's incredible career and the lessons we can draw from his journey, let's move to another dynamic and exciting player: Ronald Acuña Jr.

With his electrifying presence on the field and a stellar set of achievements, Ronald represents the next generation of baseball superstars. Let's explore the career of this phenomenal athlete and find out what makes him one of the most thrilling players in the game today.

Braves

Chapter 12

RONALD ACUÑA JR.

Stay humble, and work hard every day no matter what happens.

–RONALD ACUÑA JR.

Ronald Acuña's path to MLB stardom has been built on dedication, humility, and a strong inner drive. From the time he was a little boy, he was immersed in the world of baseball, thanks to his family's deep roots in the sport. This early exposure laid the foundation for what would become an extraordinary career marked by impressive achievements and inspiring comebacks.

Ronald's story hasn't been just about the milestones he's reached; it's also been about the challenges he's overcome on the way to the top. His rise through the minor leagues, his explosive debut with the Atlanta Braves, and his return from injury present a picture of a player who simply doesn't give up.

As one of the most dynamic players in baseball today, Ronald continues to captivate fans with his electrifying performances on the field and his positive attitude off it. Let's learn his story and find out why he's one of the most talked-about players in the game today.

RONALD'S STORY

Ronald Acuña Jr. was born in La Guaira, Venezuela. His family has a strong background in the sport, both his father and his grandfather having played professionally. Growing up in such a baseball-friendly environment, Ronald was able to develop his skills and forge a strong work ethic, inspired by the achievements of his family members.

In July 2014, when he was just 16, Ronald signed with the Atlanta Braves. His raw talent and potential were immediately evident, and he quickly rose through the ranks of the Braves' minor league system as an international free agent.

By 2017, Ronald's excellent playing earned him the title of Minor League Player of the Year, establishing him as one of the most promising prospects in baseball. During his time in the minors, he showed off his speed, power, and defensive skills, which caught the attention of baseball scouts and fans alike.

Ronald made his MLB debut with the Braves in 2018. Wearing the number 13 jersey in honor of his dad, he made an impact right off the bat. In his debut game against the Cincinnati Reds, he recorded his first MLB hit and scored the game-tying run, helping the Braves secure a win. The following day, he hit a slamming home run, setting the tone for what would be a legendary rookie season. His performance throughout the year earned him the NL Rookie of the Year award, confirming his status as a rising star in the league.

In 2019, Ronald's career continued to soar. He was selected for his first All-Star game and finished the season with 41 home runs and 37 stolen bases, narrowly missing the 40-40 club—a rare achievement in baseball history (*Ronald Acuña Jr.*, 2024). His dynamic play and electrifying presence on the field made him one of the most exciting players to watch.

During the July 2021 season, Ronald suffered a torn ACL in his right knee while attempting to field a fly ball, which ended his season prematurely. The injury was a big setback, requiring extensive surgery and rehabilitation.

Despite the physical and mental toll, Ronald got through a grueling recovery process. He leaned on his family for support, especially his young sons, whose laughter and presence provided him with the motivation to stay focused on his goal to get back on the field.

Ronald made a triumphant return in 2023, delivering a historic season. He became the first player to hit 30 home runs and steal 60 bases in a single MLB season (*Ronald Acuña Jr.*, 2024). His outstanding performance that year earned him the National League MVP award, with unanimous votes, showing his dominance in the sport.

In May 2024, Ronald suffered another torn ACL, this time in his left knee, during a game against the Pittsburgh Pirates. The injury happened right when he was making a move toward third base, and his knee buckled, causing him to fall to the ground.

This second injury was a major blow for Ronald, as it will require another round of surgery and another difficult rehabilitation process. Despite the setback, Ronald remains optimistic and focused on his recovery, determined to return to peak form and continue his career.

Looking ahead, Ronald is focused on his rehab and aims to achieve even greater success in the future. He aspires to win another MVP award and hopes to lead the Braves to more victories in the seasons to come.

Off the field, Ronald's personal life reflects his dedication to family. His two sons and wife continue to be a source of strength and inspiration for him as he recovers from his latest injury. Several members of his extended family, including his cousins, Alcides Escobar, Edwin Escobar, Kelvim Escobar, and Vicente Campos, have also played Major League Baseball, and are there for him as well, as they understand the rigors of the game, and the potential for setbacks.

Ronald's story is one of great talent, strength, and dedication. His path, from a young boy in Venezuela to a celebrated MLB star, serves as an inspiration to aspiring athletes worldwide. As he continues to recover from his injury and aims for a swift return, the baseball world eagerly anticipates his return to the field, where everyone hopes he'll continue to make history.

RONALD ACUÑA JR. FUN FACTS

- Ronald Acuña Jr.'s Braves jersey was the best-selling MLB jersey in 2023, outpacing even the likes of MLB superstars Shohei Ohtani and Fernando Tatis Jr.
- Ronald's nickname, "La Bestia," comes from a viral moment in 2019 where he pounded his chest and proclaimed, "I am a beast" in Spanish after batting a game-tying home run (Sandler, 2023).

THINGS TO THINK ABOUT

- If you could create your own celebration move after scoring a goal or hitting a home run, what would it be and why?
- Is there someone in your life who inspires you to be your best? How do they influence you?

UP NEXT

Ronald Acuña Jr.'s ability to overcome setbacks and his strong dedication to the game are truly impressive. As we reflect on what's been an amazing career to date and remember the milestones he's achieved already, we're again reminded of the impact individual players can have on the sport.

Now, let's shift our focus to another outstanding player who has made a big mark in baseball: Nolan Arenado. Known for his amazing defensive skills and consistent offensive performance, Arenado has established himself as one of the top third basemen in the majors.

28

Chapter 13

NOLAN ARENADO

God has blessed me to play and that's what I'm going to do.

–NOLAN ARENADO

Nolan Arenado's career in Major League Baseball is a shining example of dedication and solid skills. Nolan's path to baseball fame, from being a high school standout to becoming one of the most celebrated third basemen in MLB history, is a tale worth telling over and over again.

His impact on the game today has been undeniable. Known for his defensive playing, he's won multiple Gold Glove awards, setting a standard for what it means to be an elite third baseman. His trade to the St. Louis Cardinals in 2021 marked a new chapter in his career, where he continued to flex his exceptional skills and show strong leadership qualities.

As we look at the details of Nolan's baseball career so far, we'll uncover the milestones and moments that define his legacy and the lessons we can draw from the path he's blazed through MLB.

NOLAN'S STORY

Nolan Arenado was born in Newport Beach, California. His upbringing in nearby Lake Forest was steeped in a mix of Cuban and Puerto Rican heritage. This diverse cultural background, coupled with a family deeply passionate about baseball, set the stage for Nolan's early and fervent love for the sport.

Nolan's older brother, Fernando Jr., played an influential role in his development as a baseball player. The two brothers spent hours working on their skills together, driven by a fierce sibling rivalry that pushed Nolan to constantly improve. This competitive environment was further supported by the presence of other athletic family members, including his younger brother Jonah, who later pursued a career in minor league baseball, and his cousin, Josh Fuentes, who also made it to the major leagues.

Nolan's talent was clear from a young age. During high school, his skills on the baseball diamond began to gain a lot of attention. Playing shortstop, he led his school to a California Interscholastic Federation Southern Section championship during his junior year, boasting a .456 batting average (*Nolan Arenado*, 2024b). His senior year was even more impressive, batting .517 with 14 doubles and five home runs, earning himself a spot on the Los Angeles Times' All-Star team (*Nolan Arenado*, 2024b). His high school playing laid a solid foundation for his future in the major leagues.

In 2009, the Colorado Rockies drafted Nolan in the second round, recognizing his great potential. Rather than pursuing a college career at Arizona State University, he chose to begin his professional career immediately. He quickly rose through the various tiers of the Rockies organization's minor league teams, becoming known for his strong defensive skills and powerful hitting. By 2011, he led the minor leagues with 122 RBIs and was named the MVP of the Arizona Fall League (*Nolan Arenado*, 2024b).

Nolan's transition to MLB was seamless. He made his debut in a game against the Arizona Diamondbacks. In his second game, he hit a home run. His defensive skills were immediately clear, earning him a Gold Glove award in his rookie season. This achievement marked the beginning of a winning streak. Nolan went on to win 10 consecutive Gold Glove awards, making him one of the best defensive third basemen in professional baseball today.

His impact wasn't just limited to his defensive capabilities. Over his years with the Rockies, he also established himself as a powerful offensive player. In 2015, he tied Bryce Harper for the National League home run title with 42 homers and led the league with 130 RBIs (*Nolan Arenado*, 2024b). His consistency at the plate and his ability to drive in runs made him a key player for the Rockies, leading the team to multiple playoff appearances.

In a big career move, Nolan was traded to the St. Louis Cardinals before the 2021 season. The transition did nothing to fade his performance; he continued to excel both offensively and defensively. Despite a dip in his performance during the 2023 season, where he had a lower batting average and fewer home runs, Nolan stayed a key part of the Cardinals' roster.

Determined to return to his peak form, he approached the 2024 season with renewed focus. Reporting to spring training leaner and more motivated, he aimed to prove his value and reclaim his place among baseball's elite.

The 2024 season saw Nolan making a strong comeback. With multiple key hits and solid defensive plays, he continued to contribute to the Cardinals' victories. Despite facing some minor injuries, he managed to stay active and effective on the field. His strong work ethic and dedication to improvement have continued to define his career, inspiring teammates and fans alike.

Off the field, Nolan's life is marked by stability and strong familial bonds. He is married and has one daughter. Nolan's personal favorite players, Adrián Beltré and former Rockies teammate Matt Holliday, show his deep respect for fellow third basemen.

Reflecting on his career in interviews, Nolan often recalls the days of his youth, when he played all kinds of different sports with friends and family. As Nolan continues to build his legacy, his path to the top of MLB stands as a source of inspiration for baseball fans across the country, reminding us of the power of dedication, and a true love for the game.

NOLAN ARENADO FUN FACTS

- Nolan drinks chocolate milk after every game, not just for the taste, but because he believes its calcium-rich benefits aid in muscle recovery. It's become a key part of his post-game routine.
- Nolan avoids eating bread almost entirely and never eats sugar after 6 pm. This strict regimen is part of what helps him stay in peak physical condition, contributing to maintaining his energy and allowing him to stay consistent on the field.

THINGS TO THINK ABOUT

- If you could make an amazing defensive play in any sport, what would it be, and why?
- Have you ever felt like you had something to prove, like Nolan Arenado? How did you handle it, and what did you learn?

UP NEXT

After exploring Nolan Arenado's inspiring journey and his unwavering dedication to excellence, it's time to shift our focus to another remarkable third baseman: Manny Machado.

Like Nolan, Manny has carved out a stellar career through a blend of extraordinary talent and relentless work ethic. His impact on the game, both defensively and offensively, has made him one of the most talked-about players in MLB today. Let's find out what makes him such a charismatic presence on the field.

Chapter 14

MANNY MACHADO

I just try to enjoy the game, play with a smile on my face, and be the best I can be.

–MANNY MACHADO

Manny Machado's baseball career has been one defined by passion, versatility, and a deep love for the game. His positive attitude and the smile he proudly takes to the field with has made him one of MLB's most dynamic players. Whether it's making a crucial out at third base, or launching a home run far into the bleachers, his great playing time and time again reveals his level of dedication and the joyful spirit he takes to the field.

As we learn Manny's story, we'll explore how his relentless pursuit of excellence and his ability to adapt and overcome challenges have made him a standout player. His path to baseball success offers us some valuable lessons in the importance of staying true to ourselves and the power of enjoying what we do and what we care about—no matter the obstacles that threaten to kick us off track. Let's learn Manny's story!

MANNY'S STORY

Manny's path to baseball stardom is a story rooted in a passion for the game, the embrace of cultural heritage, and a strong desire to be the best. Born in Hialeah, Florida, Manny grew up in Miami, a place where baseball is more than just a sport—it's a way of life.

His Dominican heritage played a big part in shaping his identity and love for the game. Raised by his mom, Rosa, and also deeply influenced by his grandfather, Francisco Nunez, Manny was surrounded by family members who taught him about the value of hard work from an early age.

Manny's early life was intertwined with baseball, a connection that was further strengthened by his relationship with his cousin, former MLB player Yonder Alonso. Although not related by blood, Alonso and Machado grew up like brothers, with their bond forged on the baseball field. Together, they brushed up on their skills, challenging each other and dreaming of one day making it to the big leagues. This level of familial support, combined with Manny's natural talent, set a strong foundation for his future success.

Manny went to Brito Miami Private School, where he quickly made a name for himself as one of the top young baseball players in the country. As a shortstop, his defensive abilities were highly impressive and were matched by his powerful hitting. By the time he was in high school, he was already considered one of the top prospects in the nation. In 2010, he got drafted by the Baltimore Orioles as the third overall pick. His dreams had finally come true.

His decision to sign with the Orioles instead of attending Florida International University marked the beginning of his professional career. He quickly rose through the ranks of the Orioles' minor league teams, where his strong arm, quick reflexes, and powerful bat continued to impress.

Manny's ascent through the minor leagues was a quick one, as he consistently showed why he was considered a top prospect for the big leagues. His progression was so rapid that by August 2012, he was called up to make his MLB debut with the Orioles. Stepping onto the field at 20 years old, for the first time as a major leaguer, he immediately made a big impression.

His rookie season was marked by his defensive mastery at third base, a position he adapted to with ease despite having primarily played shortstop before. His natural talent, combined with a strong work ethic, allowed him to excel at the hot corner, quickly becoming a key player for the Orioles.

By the end of his first full season in 2013, Manny had earned his first All-Star selection and received a Gold Glove award for his excellent playing. He led the league in doubles, showing his true offensive capabilities.

Over the next few years, Manny continued to build on his early success. In 2015, he won his second Gold Glove award and was again selected as an All-Star, further establishing himself as one of the best players in MLB. His performances drew comparisons to some of the game's all-time greats, with many seeing echoes of Hall of Famer Brooks Robinson in Machado's defensive play. His consistent excellence made him a fan favorite in Baltimore and a respected figure across the league.

In 2018, Manny's career took a turn when he was traded to the Los Angeles Dodgers. The move to the West Coast came with high expectations, as Manny joined a team with championship aspirations. He quickly adapted to his new surroundings, helping the Dodgers reach the World Series that year. Although the Dodgers fell short of winning the title, Manny's contributions were crucial, and his performance in Los Angeles reaffirmed his status as one of the game's elite players.

Following his time playing with the Dodgers, Manny entered free agency and signed a monumental 10-year, $300 million contract with the San Diego Padres in 2019 (*Manny Machado*, 2024). The deal was one of the largest in sports history at the time, a reflection of Manny's value and the Padres' commitment to building a winning team around him. His arrival in San Diego marked the beginning of a new chapter in his career, one where he'd be both a star player and a leader.

Manny's tenure with the Padres has been marked by both personal and team achievements. Despite facing challenges, including a serious injury that required surgery on his right elbow in late 2023, Manny's determination to return to form has never ceased. He worked tirelessly to regain his strength and skills. By the start of the 2024 season, Machado was back at third base, contributing both defensively and offensively, including hitting his first home run of the season in March.

Off the field, Manny's life has been equally fulfilling. In November 2014, he married his longtime girlfriend, and together, they welcomed their first child in early 2024. His role as a father and husband has become a big part of his identity, grounding him as he continues to pursue his baseball career.

Beyond baseball, Manny has also expanded his influence into other areas, including sports ownership. In 2023, he became part of the ownership group for San Diego FC, an expansion team in Major League Soccer set to begin play in 2025. This move highlights Manny's passion for sports and his desire to contribute to the San Diego community, a place that has become his home both on and off the field.

Manny's story has been one of talent, strength, and a deep love for the game of baseball. From his early days in Miami to his rise as one of the most respected players in Major League Baseball, Manny has consistently shown a commitment to being the best he can be.

MANNY MACHADO FUN FACTS

- In 2018, Manny logged his 1,000th career hit during his time playing with the Dodgers. He was one of the youngest players to achieve this number.
- Manny is a huge fan of the late basketball legend Kobe Bryant. His admiration for Bryant is so deep that he named his dog Kobe!

THINGS TO THINK ABOUT

- How would you balance school and sports if you were an athlete, like Machado balancing his family and baseball?
- What is one skill you would like to perfect in your favorite sport, and how would you practice it?

UP NEXT

After learning about Manny Machado's impressive contributions to the world of baseball, it's now time to turn our attention to another towering figure in the sport: Gerrit Cole.

Known for his commanding presence on the pitcher's mound, Gerrit's career offers a wealth of lessons in determination and leadership. As we explore his story, we'll discover the qualities that have made him one of the most dominant pitchers in the game today, and how his impact reaches far beyond the diamond.

H
HOUSTON
45

Chapter 15

GERRIT COLE

Trying to get better, always, is my goal.

–GERRIT COLE

Gerrit Cole's rise to the top of MLB is a story of constant improvement. This, along with a positive mindset, has helped him throughout his career, from his early days as a young pitcher in California to his emergence as one of the most dominant forces on the mound.

Gerrit's journey isn't just about natural talent; it's about an unwavering commitment to refining his craft and overcoming setbacks. His story is one of striving to be the best, making him a true inspiration for anyone who understands the value of dedication and measured progress. Let's learn his story.

GERRIT'S STORY

Gerrit was born in Newport Beach, California. He grew up in nearby Tustin, where baseball became more than just a pastime for him. His dad, Mark, was key in encouraging Gerrit's love for the game. They spent countless hours playing catch together. Gerrit's mother, Sharon, was equally supportive, ensuring that her son balanced his baseball obsession with his schoolwork.

By the time he was in high school, Gerrit's talent was undeniable. He went to Orange Lutheran High School, where he made headlines as a standout pitcher. His fastball, which clocked in at 94 miles per hour by his junior year, caught the attention of scouts from across the country (*Gerrit Cole*, 2024)!

Gerrit's senior year was one for the record books. His fastball consistently clocked in at 96 miles per hour, and he finished the season with an 8-2 record and a remarkable 0.47 ERA, striking out 121 batters in just 75 innings (*Gerrit Cole*, 2024). His performance led to him being named to *USA Today*'s All-USA High School Baseball Team and established him as one of the top high school prospects in the entire country.

He was drafted by the New York Yankees in 2008, but decided to go to college instead of jumping straight into the pros. This decision, guided by his desire to further develop both as a player and a person, led him to UCLA, where he would be able to refine his skills and prepare for the challenges of the major leagues.

Gerrit's time in college ball was marked by rapid development and increasing recognition as one of the top pitchers in college baseball. From the outset, he was a key player for the UCLA Bruins, earning the coveted role of Friday night starter during his freshman year—a clear sign that his coaches had a lot of trust in him.

Gerrit's freshman year was impressive, but it was during his sophomore and junior years that he truly began to dominate. Alongside fellow future MLB pitcher Trevor Bauer, Gerrit helped lead the Bruins to a 51-17 record in 2010, the best in the school's history (*Gerrit Cole*, 2024). That year, UCLA made it all the way to the College World Series, finishing as the national runner-up.

In his sophomore season, Gerrit posted an 11-4 record with a 3.37 ERA and struck out 153 batters in 123 innings, placing him among the top collegiate pitchers in the country (*Gerrit Cole*, 2024). His junior year, though statistically less dominant, did nothing to diminish his chances in the MLB draft. His reputation as a power pitcher with a fastball that regularly touched the upper 90s and a devastating slider made him one of the most coveted prospects.

The Pittsburgh Pirates, recognizing his potential to be a franchise-altering talent, selected Gerrit as their first overall draft pick in 2011. He signed a record-breaking $8 million signing bonus, the largest ever for a rookie at the time (*Gerrit Cole*, 2024). This marked the beginning of Cole's professional path, as he prepared to navigate the challenging road ahead of him, from a highly touted prospect to a major league star.

After working on his skills in the minor leagues, he made his much-anticipated MLB debut with the Pittsburgh Pirates. Against the San Francisco Giants in his first game, Gerrit wasted no time making an impact. He struck out the first player up to bat and hit a two-run single in his first at-bat. Gerrit pitched 6.1 innings, allowing just two earned runs, and earned the win (*Gerrit Cole*, 2024). Gerrit's first game in the pros set the tone for what would be a promising rookie season.

Gerrit's performance throughout his rookie year was awesome. In September 2013, he was named the NL Rookie of the Month after posting a 4-0 record with a 1.69 ERA and 39 strikeouts (*Gerrit Cole*, 2024). He finished his rookie season with a 10-7 record and a 3.22 ERA, quickly establishing himself as a key figure in the Pirates' rotation (*Gerrit Cole*, 2024). Gerrit's efforts helped bring the Pirates to their first postseason appearance in over two decades, where he delivered a standout performance in the National League Division Series.

In January 2018, the Pirates made a franchise-altering decision by trading Gerrit to the Houston Astros. This move would prove to be a pivotal moment in Gerrit's career, as the Astros, known for their analytical approach to pitching, helped him unlock a new level of performance. In Houston, he became one of the most dominant pitchers in the game, transforming from a promising young arm into a bona fide ace.

Under the guidance of the Astros' coaching staff, Cole refined his pitch selection and mechanics, focusing on throwing more high-velocity fastballs and increasing his spin rate. The results were immediate and dramatic. In 2018, Cole struck out a career-high 276 batters, posting a 15-5 record with a 2.88 ERA (*Gerrit Cole*, 2024). His performance earned him his first All-Star selection as a member of the American League.

The following season, Gerrit's continued dominance on the mound was a key factor in the Astros' 2019 World Series playoffs run, where they ultimately fell in seven games to the Washington Nationals. Despite the loss, Cole's 2019 season was historic.

Gerrit's success in Houston set the stage for one of the most lucrative free-agent contracts in MLB history. In December 2019, he signed a $324 million contract with the New York Yankees for nine years, making him the highest-paid pitcher in the history of the sport at that time (*Gerrit Cole*, 2024). The Yankees, who had long been interested in Gerrit, viewed him as the missing piece in their quest for another World Series title.

Gerrit's first season with the Yankees in 2020 was unique, as it was shortened by the COVID-19 pandemic. Despite the stress of playing under uncertain conditions, he lived up to the hype around him, posting a 7-3 record with a 2.84 ERA and 94 strikeouts in 73 innings (*Gerrit Cole*, 2024). He quickly became the ace of the Yankees' pitching staff, known for his competitive fire and meticulous preparation. Cole's presence on the mound brought a level of stability and confidence to the team, and he quickly endeared himself to the Yankees' passionate fan base.

The peak of Gerrit's career came in 2022 when he was finally awarded the AL Cy Young Award. He finished the season with a 2.63 ERA, 222 strikeouts, and 15 wins (*Gerrit Cole*, 2024). His ability to dominate hitters with a mix of high-velocity fastballs, sharp sliders, and precise control made him nearly unhittable.

In 2024, Gerrit faced one of the most challenging periods of his career when he was sidelined with elbow nerve inflammation. This injury required a 60-day stint on the injured list, a significant setback for both Cole and the Yankees. However, true to his nature, Gerrit approached his rehabilitation with the same intensity and focus that had defined his career. He made several starts in the minor leagues, gradually building up his strength and pitch count in preparation for his return to the majors.

Gerrit's return to the Yankees' rotation in June 2024 was met with anticipation and relief. While his initial outings were not without challenges, his presence alone was a boost to the team. His first start back, against the Baltimore Orioles, saw him strike out five batters over four innings, a solid performance after months of rehab.

Off the field, Gerrit Cole's life is anchored by his family. His wife is a former college softball star. They have two kids together, and Gerrit often speaks about the importance of family in his life.

Despite his success and massive fortune, Gerrit is still grounded and connected to his roots. He still drives a 2006 Toyota pickup truck that his dad bought for him in high school, a symbol of his humble beginnings and the values instilled in him by his parents.

GERRIT COLE FUN FACTS

- Gerrit's dad was from New York, and they're both lifelong Yankees fans. In 2001, a young Gerrit Cole was photographed at the World Series holding a sign that read, "Yankee fan today tomorrow forever." The photo went viral when Cole signed with the Yankees in 2019 (*Gerrit Cole*, 2024).
- He loves to cook and is a talented musician. He can play both piano and guitar.

THINGS TO THINK ABOUT

- If you were an MLB pitcher like Gerrit Cole, which injury would you fear the most? Why?
- What qualities do you think are important for being a good leader on a sports team? How does Gerrit show strong leadership?

UP NEXT

Now having learned about Gerrit's awesomc baseball career and his impact on MLB, we can take a moment to step back and appreciate the dedication and skill required to reach the top of the game.

In the next chapter, we turn our attention to another standout pitcher who has made his mark with his unique style and undeniable talent: Marcus Stroman. His path to baseball success has been equally compelling. Let's explore how Stroman has become a dominant force in baseball while carving out his own distinct legacy.

C

Chapter 16

MARCUS STROMAN

Be better today than you were yesterday.

–MARCUS STROMAN

Despite facing countless challenges and working hard to overcome doubts about his abilities due to his height, Marcus Stroman has carved out a remarkable career as one of the sport's most dynamic pitchers.

His story isn't just about athletic success; it's about proving that heart, determination, and a commitment to self-improvement can help us defy the expectations of others. As we start to learn about Marcus' life and career, we'll explore how these principles have shaped him into the top-notch athlete he is today. Let's learn his story.

MARCUS' STORY

Born in Medford, New York, Marcus was introduced to the game of baseball at a young age. Growing up in a diverse and supportive family environment, he was driven by a strong work ethic instilled in him by his parents. His dad, Earl, and his mom, Adlin, both played important roles in shaping his character and passion for the sport.

Marcus' talent in baseball was clear from the time he was young. He went to Patchogue-Medford High School, where he became a standout athlete. During his high school years, he developed a fierce rivalry and friendship with future MLB pitcher Steven Matz, who would later be his teammate on the New York Mets. The two often pitched against each other in high school, with their matchups drawing attention from scouts across Major League Baseball. Stroman's performances on the mound, characterized by his blazing fastball and sharp breaking pitches, quickly made him a top prospect.

Even though he was drafted by the Washington Nationals in 2009, Marcus chose not to sign right away. Instead, he decided to go to Duke University, where he could further develop his skills. He quickly became one of the top collegiate pitchers in the country. At Duke, he set school records for strikeouts and showed his versatility by also playing second base and shortstop.

He first made waves on the 2011 U.S.A. Collegiate National Team, where he had an amazing 0.00 ERA throughout seven games, striking out 17 batters (*Six Things to Know about Marcus Stroman*, n.d.).

Marcus' success at Duke led to him being drafted by the Toronto Blue Jays in 2012. He first played with the Vancouver Canadians, but his rapid development allowed him to quickly get called up to the AA New Hampshire Fisher Cats.

In 2012, he faced a 50-game suspension for testing positive for a banned stimulant, which he claimed to have unknowingly consumed in an over-the-counter supplement. This incident did not deter him though. He returned stronger, using the experience as fuel to propel his career forward.

In 2014, Marcus made his MLB debut with the Toronto Blue Jays, and he quickly established himself as a reliable starter in their rotation. His rookie season was marked by some impressive performances, including his first complete game and shutout against the Chicago Cubs. His ability to stay composed and deliver in high-pressure situations became a hallmark of his playing style. Marcus continued working toward his degree while he played, and eventually graduated from Duke with a bachelor's degree in sociology in 2016.

Marcus' baseball career reached new heights in 2017 when he helped Team USA win the World Baseball Classic championship. In the final game, he held Team Puerto Rico scoreless and without a hit through six innings, earning him the MVP award.

In 2019, Marcus was traded to the New York Mets, where he continued to be an impactful pitcher. He quickly became a fan favorite. However, after the 2021 season, he started to seek out new opportunities, signing a three-year deal with the Chicago Cubs in 2022. His time with the Cubs was marked by solid performances, and he was selected for the All-team in 2023.

Marcus' journey came full circle in January 2024 when he signed a two-year deal with the New York Yankees. This move was particularly significant for Stroman, as it marked his return to New York, fulfilling his lifelong dream of playing for the Bronx Bombers. His early performances with the Yankees in the 2024 season were strong, as he delivered multiple quality starts, proving that his passion for the game and his determination to succeed had only grown stronger with time.

Beyond the field, Marcus' personal life is rich with meaning and symbolism. He has several tattoos, each representing significant aspects of his life and heritage. From his grandma to the area code of his hometown to portraits of his parents, and quotes that inspire him daily, his tattoos tell the story of a player who's still deeply connected to his roots, his family, and his identity.

MARCUS STROMAN FUN FACTS

- Standing at just 5' 7", Marcus has always defied the odds in sports. To inspire other short kings, he created the mantra "Height Doesn't Measure Heart" (HDMH). Aside from becoming his personal philosophy, it also inspired the name of his clothing line, HDMH Apparel.
- Marcus' jersey bears the number 6 in honor of his grandmother, whose birthday is on March 6.
- His younger brother, Jayden, is also a rising baseball talent.

THINGS TO THINK ABOUT

- Imagine people telling you that you couldn't achieve your dreams because of something you can't change, like your height. How would you prove them wrong?
- If you were a famous athlete, what cause would you support in your community and how would you make a difference?

UP NEXT

After learning about Marcus Stroman's remarkable journey, from his rise in MLB to overcoming challenges with determination and heart, it's now time to turn our focus to another exceptional talent in baseball: Mookie Betts.

Like Marcus, Mookie has made a big impact on the game, not just through his athletic excellence, but also through his leadership and dedication. Let's find out how Mookie managed to become one of today's top players.

LA
Dodgers

Chapter 17

MOOKIE BETTS

My Mom and Dad always told me to not act on emotion, act on what is real. When you're mad don't do something wrong because you're mad.

–MOOKIE BETTS

Mookie Betts' baseball career has been shaped by a strong foundation built on the values imparted by his parents, especially the wisdom of not letting emotions dictate actions. This approach has not only allowed him to navigate the intense pressures of professional sports but has also contributed to his success on and off the field.

In this chapter, we'll find out how his exceptional versatility and focus have helped him become one of the most respected and admired players in Major League Baseball. From his early days in Nashville to his rise as an MVP and World Series champion, Mookie's story is a shining example of how staying grounded and acting on what is real can lead to extraordinary achievements.

MOOKIE'S STORY

Born Markus Lynn Betts in Nashville, Tennessee, from the time he was young, Mookie exhibited a natural athleticism that set him apart. Growing up in a sports-centric family, he was encouraged to pursue his passions, which, aside from baseball, included basketball and bowling. His mom, recognizing his talent, became one of his earliest and most dedicated coaches, even forming a Little League team so her son could play when others doubted his potential due to his small height.

At John Overton High School, Mookie's abilities became apparent across multiple sports. On the baseball field, he was a force to be reckoned with, earning praise and drawing the attention of college scouts and professional teams. He batted .548 with 24 steals in his junior year, showing his speed and precision (*Mookie Betts*, 2024). Mookie also excelled in basketball, earning MVP honors in the District 12-AAA league during his senior year.

In 2010, he became Tennessee's Boys Bowler of the Year in 2010 after scoring 290—just 10 pins shy of a perfect game (*10 Things You Didn't Know about Mookie Betts*, 2015)! Despite his talents in multiple sports, he chose to pursue baseball.

In 2011, Mookie got drafted by the Boston Red Sox. Although he had a scholarship offer from the University of Tennessee, he ultimately chose to sign with the Sox, a decision that would lead to his rapid rise through the minor leagues.

From the start, Mookie wowed crowds with his speed, defense, and hitting ability. His brief minor league stint with the Pawtucket Red Socks was marked by consistent improvement and adaptation. By 2013, Mookie was on the radar as one of Boston's most promising prospects, and it wasn't long before he would make his mark on the major leagues.

Mookie made his MLB debut with the Red Sox in 2014, and it was immediately clear that he was a special player. His combination of speed, defensive versatility, and batting power earned him a regular spot in the lineup. By the time the 2015 season rolled around, Mookie was widely recognized as one of the most exciting young players in the game. His ability to make spectacular plays in the outfield and his knack for scoring runs made him a key player for the Red Sox.

The peak of Mookie's career with the Red Sox came in 2018, a season that will go down in history as one of the best individual performances in baseball. Mookie won the AL MVP award, leading the league with a .346 batting average, 129 runs scored, and a .640 slugging percentage (*Mookie Betts*, 2024). Mookie also became a member of the prestigious 30-30 club, hitting 32 home runs and stealing 30 bases (*Mookie Betts*, 2024). That year, Mookie led the Red Sox to a World Series championship.

In 2020, after six seasons with the Red Sox, Mookie got traded to the Los Angeles Dodgers in a blockbuster deal. The Dodgers, recognizing his immense value, signed him to a 12-year, $365 million contract extension, making him one of the highest-paid players in MLB history (*Mookie Betts*, 2024).

Mookie wasted no time in making an impact in Los Angeles. In his first season with the Dodgers, he helped bring the team to a World Series title, their first in 32 years. His contributions both at the plate and in the field were instrumental to the Dodgers' success, and he quickly became a fan favorite in Los Angeles.

Throughout his career, Mookie has shown an extraordinary ability to play multiple positions. Initially a second baseman, Mookie transitioned to the outfield, where he became one of the best defensive right fielders in the game. His versatility was put on full display in the 2024 season when he took on the challenge of playing shortstop, a position he hadn't played since his minor league days.

Despite the challenges of adapting to a new position, Mookie thrived, earning praise for his defensive abilities and continuing to produce offensively.

The 2024 season kicked off on a high note for Mookie, as he was named the NL Player of the Month for April after a scorching start at the plate. He started off the season leading the league in several offensive categories and celebrated his 1,500th career hit, but his momentum was abruptly halted in June when he suffered a fractured left hand after being hit by a pitch. Despite this setback, Mookie remains optimistic, focusing on his recovery and determined to return to the field as soon as possible.

Off the field, Mookie Betts is known for his humility, work ethic, and strong family ties. He married his high school sweetheart, Brianna Hammonds, in 2021, and the couple has built a life together that includes their young daughter. He's still an accomplished bowler, having bowled multiple perfect games and competed in professional tournaments. His love for bowling is just one example of his diverse talents and interests, which go way beyond the baseball diamond.

Mookie's impact on the game of baseball goes beyond his statistics and accolades. He stands as a role model for young athletes, showing that hard work, versatility, and a positive attitude can lead to success both on and off the field. His journey from a small kid in Nashville to one of the biggest stars in Major League Baseball is an inspiration to all who face challenges and doubters along the way.

MOOKIE BETTS FUN FACTS

- Mookie comes from a family with deep baseball roots. His uncle, Terry Shumpert, played 14 seasons in the Major Leagues.

- Mookie Betts' full name is Markus Lynn Betts. His mom chose these names intentionally to give him the initials "MLB," knowing that one day he'd grow up to be a baseball star.

THINGS TO THINK ABOUT

- If you were Mookie's mom, what name would you choose for him to have the initials "MLB?"
- What are your top two favorite sports? Which one would you choose?

UP NEXT

After finding out all about Mookie Betts' impressive contributions to baseball and his influential presence beyond the diamond, let's turn our attention to another outstanding athlete in baseball today: Cody Bellinger.

Known for his powerful swing and versatility on the field, Cody has carved out his own place in MLB history. His path to greatness, filled with remarkable highs and challenges, exemplifies the determination required to succeed at the highest level of the sport. Let's explore the career of this exceptional player who continues to leave his mark on the game.

35

Chapter 18

CODY BELLINGER

I'm up here to help the team win every at-bat, offense, defense, baserunning.

– CODY BELLINGER

Cody Bellinger is more than just a name on the roster; he's a force to be reckoned with in Major League Baseball today. Known for his powerful swing, his versatility on the field, and his ability to rise to the occasion when it matters most, Cody's playing has captured the attention of baseball fans and analysts.

As we learn how Cody made it to the top, we'll explore the moments that have defined his path in baseball and the qualities that have made him one of the most compelling players of his generation. Let's learn his story.

CODY'S STORY

Born in Scottsdale, Arizona, Cody grew up in a family where baseball was more than just a sport—it was a way of life. His dad, Clay, was an MLB player himself, one who had three World Series championships with the New York Yankees under his belt. Growing up with a baseball-champion dad, Cody was exposed to the game from a very young age, and soon, he started to pick up his own set of athletic abilities.

Cody played Little League Baseball as a youngster. When he was 11, he helped lead his team to the 2007 Little League World Series, an experience that would foreshadow his future success on bigger stages. This early exposure to high-pressure games helped shape his mental toughness and fueled his ambition to pursue his own career in baseball.

Cody went to Hamilton High School in Chandler, Arizona, where he continued to develop his skills. He was a standout player in baseball and also became known as a multi-sport athlete. During his senior year, he was the team MVP and batted an impressive .429 (*Cody Bellinger*, 2024). Though he was very tall (6' 4"), he only weighed 170 pounds. His potential was undeniable. Scouts took notice of his smooth swing and defensive skills, even though his power-hitting ability had yet to fully develop.

In the 2013 MLB Draft, the Los Angeles Dodgers selected Cody in the fourth round. Although he had committed to playing college baseball for the Oregon Ducks, he chose to sign with the Dodgers, kicking off his professional career. He spent his first few years in the minor leagues, where his talent began to blossom. After struggling initially at the plate, he made some adjustments that allowed him to gain a competitive edge on the field. By 2015, he was playing for the Rancho Cucamonga Quakes and was named the MVP of the California League Championship Series, helping his team secure the title.

Cody's rise through the minor leagues was meteoric. In 2017, after a brief stint with the Oklahoma City Dodgers, he was called up to the majors. His impact was immediate—Cody took the league by storm, setting multiple rookie records, including the most home runs by a National League rookie in a single season, with 39 (*Cody Bellinger*, 2024). His stellar performance earned him the NL Rookie of the Year award.

In 2019, Cody reached new heights, winning the National League MVP award. That season, he hit 47 home runs, drove in 115 runs, and maintained a .305 batting average (*Cody Bellinger*, 2024). His all-around performance, both offensively and defensively, established him as one of the premier players in the game. Cody was also a key figure in the Dodgers' World Series run in 2020, helping the team capture their first title since 1988. His home run in Game 7 of the NLCS against the Atlanta Braves was a defining moment, showing he had what it took to perform under pressure.

The years following his MVP season were interrupted by injuries. In 2021, he suffered a series of setbacks, including a fractured fibula and a dislocated shoulder, which affected his performance. His batting average plummeted, and he struggled to regain the form that had made him one of the most feared hitters in the game. Despite these challenges, Cody's will to keep playing as hard as he could never faded. He continued to work on his game, determined to return to his previous level of playing.

In 2023, after becoming a free agent, Cody signed a one-year contract with the Chicago Cubs. This move marked a new chapter in his career, and he seized the opportunity to prove himself once again. With the Cubs, he batted .307 with 26 home runs and 97 RBIs, earning the National League Comeback Player of the Year award (Bastian, 2024). His awesome performance in the 2023 season convinced the Cubs to offer him a three-year, $80 million contract extension in 2024, ensuring that he remained a key figure in their lineup (Bastian, 2024).

Cody's versatility on the field has been a big asset throughout his entire career. Known especially for his defensive skills, he has seamlessly transitioned between center field and first base, providing his teams with valuable flexibility. This ability to play well at different positions, combined with his power at the plate, has made him one of the most well-rounded players in the league.

Off the field, Cody has embraced his role as a father. He and his girlfriend, model Chase Carter, have two daughters, born in November 2021 and April 2023. From his early days in Little League to his rise as an MVP and World Series champion, Cody has proved that he has the drive and determination to overcome any obstacle.

As he continues his career with the Chicago Cubs, fans can expect Cody to keep making headlines with his powerful batting, awesome defense skills, and strong commitment to the game.

CODY BELLINGER FUN FACTS

- Unlike many MLB power hitters, Cody wasn't known for his hitting when he was younger. In fact, he hit only one home run during his senior year of high school! It wasn't until he adjusted his swing in the minor leagues that he became the home run slugger we know today.
- Cody made a cameo appearance in the video game *Assassin's Creed Valhalla*, where a character inspired by him uses a tree branch as a baseball bat!

THINGS TO THINK ABOUT

- If you could play multiple positions in your favorite sport, which ones would you choose and why?

- Do you want to do what your parents do, like how Cody became a baseball player because his dad was one? Or do you want to do something else?

UP NEXT

After learning about Cody Bellinger's life and baseball career, let's turn our attention to another exceptional player: Vladimir Guerrero Jr.

Much like Cody, Vladimir has lived up to some steep expectations set by his family legacy while carving out his own unique place in baseball history. As the son of a Hall of Famer, Vladimir carries a name that resonates deeply within the sport, and like Cody, his personal achievements have ensured that he's recognized on his own merits.

BLUE JAYS

Chapter 19

VLADIMIR GUERRERO JR.

Last year was the trailer. Now you guys are going to see the movie.

–VLADIMIR GUERRERO JR.

Vladimir Guerrero Jr. is no stranger to high expectations. Born into baseball royalty as the son of Hall of Famer Vladimir Guerrero Sr., he was destined to follow in the footsteps of his legendary father.

As we learn Vladimir Jr.'s story, we'll find out how this young superstar emerged as a powerhouse in the sport, blending his inherited talent with his own unique flair. From his early days in the Dominican Republic to his meteoric rise through the minor leagues and his spectacular breakout season, Vladimir Jr.'s journey is about a constant desire to be the best.

This chapter uncovers the pivotal moments in Vladimir Jr.'s career, the influence of his dad, and the lessons he's learned along the way as he continues to carve out his own path in the sport.

VLADIMIR'S STORY

Vladimir Guerrero Jr. was born in Montreal, Canada, while his dad, Vladimir Guerrero Sr., was playing for the Montreal Expos.

Growing up in the shadow of a Hall of Famer, baseball was a big part of Vladimir Jr.'s life from the very beginning. Even though he was born in Montreal, he spent much of his childhood in the Dominican Republic, where he was raised by his mother, Riquelma Ramos, and guided by his uncle, Wilton Guerrero, another former Major League Baseball player.

The Dominican Republic is a country that lives and breathes baseball, and it was the perfect place for young Vladimir's talent to blossom. It was there, under the watchful eyes of his father and uncle, that his love for the game deepened and his natural skills started to develop.

By the time he was 16, Vladimir was already on the radar of MLB scouts as one of the most promising young talents in international baseball. His potential was undeniable, drawing the attention of the Toronto Blue Jays, who saw in him the makings of a future star.

In 2015, the Blue Jays signed Guerrero as an international free agent with a $3.9 million signing bonus, a big sum for a teenager whose pedigree and raw talent were expected to translate into major league success (*Vladimir Guerrero Jr.*, 2024). This marked the beginning of a journey that would see him rise rapidly through the ranks of the Blue Jays organization, carrying the weight of his famous last name with both pride and determination.

Vladimir's ascent through the minor leagues was thrilling to witness. From the moment he made his professional debut, his playing had the same raw power and exceptional hitting ability that had made his father a legend. In 2016, playing for the Bluefield Blue Jays, he immediately made an impact, proving his prodigious power at the plate.

Vladimir Jr.'s performances earned him a reputation as one of the most exciting prospects in baseball. By 2017, he was a standout with the Lansing Lugnuts, where he was named a Midwest League

All-Star. He continued to rise as he moved through the minor league system, consistently delivering impressive stats. In 2018, he was named Minor League Player of the Year by *USA Today* and *Baseball America* after batting an astounding .381 with 20 home runs, a clear sign that he was ready for the big leagues (*Vladimir Guerrero Jr.*, 2024).

The long-anticipated moment came on April 26, 2019, when Vladimir made his MLB debut with the Toronto Blue Jays. The baseball world watched as the son of a Hall of Famer took his first steps onto the major league stage. In his first game, he provided glimpses of his immense potential, and it wasn't long before he hit his stride. Just a few weeks after his debut, Vladimir hit his first major league home run, a powerful shot that announced his arrival in the big leagues. This was just the beginning, as he continued to show the same level of performance that had characterized his minor league career, earning him a place among the game's most promising young stars.

The 2021 season was a defining year for Vladimir, as he fulfilled the expectations placed upon him. In a season that saw him hit 48 home runs, tying for the most in the league, he emerged as one of the best hitters in baseball. His home runs, along with 123 runs scored and 363 total bases, propelled the Blue Jays into playoff contention and made him a leading contender for the American League MVP award. Although he ultimately finished as the runner-up, his performance proved his talent and work ethic.

Vladimir's consistent excellence has been recognized with multiple All-Star selections. By 2024, he had been named to the All-Star team four times, a reflection of his sustained impact on the game. With his 2021 All-Star Game MVP award, he became the youngest player ever to win the honor. This recognition, combined with his regular season achievements, made it clear that Vladimir wasn't just living up to the legacy of his father, but was also carving out his own place in the annals of baseball history.

Vladimir has continued to make headlines with his record-setting arbitration win in 2024, securing a $19.9 million salary for the season (*Vladimir Guerrero Jr.*, 2024). The 2024 season began with a powerful reassertion of his merit. On Opening Day, he launched a whopping 450-foot home run, a reminder of the raw power that he brings to the plate. This towering shot set the tone for what would be another standout season for Vladimir, who continued to be a cornerstone of the Blue Jays' offense. His ability to deliver in key moments of the game has made him an important figure in the team's lineup and a player that opposing pitchers fear.

Beyond his achievements on the field, Vladimir remains deeply connected to his roots and his family. He's known for his close relationship with his grandma, who played a big part in his upbringing and has been a constant presence in his life.

Vladimir's strong family ties are a testament to his grounded nature, despite his rising stardom. He is also a devout Christian, and his faith plays an important role in his life, guiding him both personally and professionally. Off the field, he has shown that he's committed to giving back to the community, especially through initiatives that support youth baseball programs, ensuring that the next generation has the same opportunities that he had, even if they didn't grow up baseball royalty like he did.

VLADIMIR GUERRERO JR. FUN FACTS

- Fluent in both Spanish and English, Guerrero Jr. uses his bilingual abilities to connect with a diverse range of teammates and fans, making him a beloved figure in the baseball community.

- Vladimir Jr. was the cover athlete of the baseball video game *MLB The Show 24*. His dad had previously been on the cover of *MLB 2006*, making the father-son duo the first to both appear on the cover of an MLB video game series (*Vladimir Guerrero Jr.*, 2024).

THINGS TO THINK ABOUT

- If you could hit a baseball as far as Vladimir Guerrero Jr., where would you want your home run to land and why?
- How has your family supported you in your favorite activities, just like Vladimir's family has supported him in baseball?

UP NEXT

After exploring Vladimir Guerrero Jr.'s impressive accomplishments, it's time to shift our focus to another powerhouse in the world of baseball: Giancarlo Stanton.

With a reputation for launching towering home runs and a presence at the plate that strikes fear into the hearts of pitchers, Giancarlo is known as one of the best hitters in the game today. He has repeatedly shown the ability to rise to the occasion when it matters most. Let's get ready to meet a player whose impact on the game has been as slamming as his home runs.

Chapter 20

GIANCARLO STANTON

I do what I love every day.

–GIANCARLO STANTON

Giancarlo Stanton is a player who has faced numerous challenges and setbacks in his career, yet he continues to rise above them. His baseball career has largely been about his deep love for the game and his commitment to playing as hard as he can. Giancarlo's path to becoming one of Major League Baseball's most powerful hitters is a story of raw talent and intense dedication.

As we learn his story, we'll explore the highs and lows, from his early days as a standout athlete in California to his current role as a key figure in the New York Yankees' lineup. Let's take a closer look at the life and career of Giancarlo, a player who exemplifies the power of doing what you love every day. Let's learn his story.

GIANCARLO'S STORY

Born in Panorama City, California, Giancarlo grew up in Los Angeles. His athletic abilities were strong from a young age, and he played many different sports during his high school years at Notre Dame High School in Sherman Oaks. Giancarlo wasn't just a standout in baseball; he also was great at basketball and football.

In 2007, when he was only 17, Giancarlo was drafted by the Miami Marlins. Opting to forgo college, he signed the deal, beginning his professional baseball career. His ascent through the minor leagues was rapid, fueled by his extraordinary power and natural ability at the plate.

By 2010, Giancarlo made his MLB debut with the Marlins, instantly making an impact with his prodigious home run power. His ability to hit towering home runs quickly earned him a reputation as one of the most exciting young players to watch.

Giancarlo's breakout came in 2017, a year that would define his career. That season, he led Major League Baseball with an astounding 59 home runs and 132 RBIs, achievements that earned him the National League MVP award (*Giancarlo Stanton*, 2024). His monstrous home runs, often exceeding 450 feet, became a regular spectacle, and his performances firmed up his status as one of the game's best players (*Giancarlo Stanton*, 2024).

Following his MVP season, Giancarlo was traded to the New York Yankees in December 2017. The move to the Bronx brought heightened expectations, and Giancarlo continued to display his immense power at the plate, hitting multiple home runs that ranked among the hardest hit.

Despite his success, Giancarlo's career with the Yankees has been interrupted by several injuries. These have included hamstring strains and knee issues, which have limited his playing time and disrupted his rhythm. However, he has stayed committed to rehab efforts, continually working to return to peak form each time.

In 2024, Giancarlo entered the season with renewed focus and determination. After enduring a challenging 2023 season, he revamped his training regimen, shedding weight and improving his mobility in an effort to regain his MVP form. This commitment to his fitness and performance quickly paid off, as he started the 2024 season with a series of powerful performances, including a 119.9 mph home run—one of the hardest-hit balls in MLB that year (*119.9 Mph! Stanton's Huge HR the Hardest Hit in MLB This Year*, 2024). His ability to bounce back from setbacks and maintain his place as one of baseball's most feared hitters speaks volumes about his work ethic and dedication.

Off the field, Giancarlo is known for his strong work ethic, a trait instilled in him by his father, a retired postal worker who had a helping hand in Giancarlo's development as an athlete. Though Giancarlo likes to keep his personal life under wraps, he is currently single, as reported by the online magazine *HOLA!* (Gomez, 2024).

GIANCARLO STANTON FUN FACTS

- Throughout high school, his minor league years, and his first two years of major league, he was known as Mike Stanton, but declared that he preferred his first name, Giancarlo, after a trip to Europe.
- Giancarlo is known for his impressive physical stature, standing 6 feet 6 inches tall and weighing 245 pounds.
- Giancarlo Stanton holds the record for the hardest-hit home run in MLB history: 121.7mph in 2018 and 121.3mph in 2020.

THINGS TO THINK ABOUT

- Giancarlo Stanton's emphasis on physical strength and training highlights the importance of fitness and preparation in achieving athletic excellence.

- Giancarlo's ability to handle pressure and perform in high-stakes situations shows the value of staying calm and focused under pressure.

BACK TO THE DUGOUT

Now that we've learned the stories and achievements of baseball's rising stars, let's reflect on the lessons we've learned and how they can apply to our own lives.

CONCLUSION

As we come to the end of this journey through the lives of baseball's rising stars, it's time to reflect on the powerful lessons these stories have shared. Each player featured in this book faced their own unique set of challenges, whether it was battling injuries, overcoming doubts due to their size or background, or navigating the pressures of living up to enormous expectations. What unites them is not just their extraordinary talent but their passion for the game.

From Aaron Judge's towering home runs and leadership on and off the field to Shohei Ohtani's groundbreaking success as both a pitcher and a hitter, we've seen that greatness in baseball doesn't come from talent alone. It's built on a foundation of hard work, sticktoitiveness, and a positive mindset. Mike Trout's consistency, Freddie Freeman's resilience through personal loss, and Bryce Harper's commitment to being a role model off the field remind us that character is as important as skill.

These athletes have faced setbacks that might have ended the careers of others, yet they've found ways to rise above. Clayton Kershaw's battles with injuries, Max Scherzer's fierce determination to honor his brother's memory, and José Altuve's defiance of the odds stacked against him due to his height—all these stories show that challenges are not roadblocks but opportunities to grow stronger.

As you've read through these inspiring stories, you've hopefully seen that the road to success isn't always smooth. It's filled with ups and downs, triumphs and tribulations. But remember that each one of these players has shown us that with the right attitude, we can overcome any obstacle. They didn't give up when things got tough, and neither should you.

Whether you dream of playing in the major leagues, excelling in another sport, or pursuing a completely different passion, the lessons these players have taught us can apply to any goal. Hard work, team playing, and a positive mindset are the keys to success, no matter what path you choose.

The stories in this book are just the beginning. Each of these players is part of a larger history that has shaped the game of baseball over the years. If you're inspired by what you've read, I encourage you to learn more about these players and the rich history of baseball. Visit the Baseball Hall of Fame, watch classic games, read more books about the sport, and dive into the statistics and stories that make baseball such an incredible game.

The world of baseball is vast and filled with even more stories of triumph, innovation, and inspiration. Whether it's learning about the legendary players who came before or following the current stars as they continue to make history, there's always something new to discover.

Now that you've learned the inspiring stories behind some of today's rising baseball stars, it's your turn to hit one out of the park! Keep dreaming big, stay determined, and remember—you can achieve anything you set your mind to. Whether you're stepping up to the plate in a real game or tackling challenges in school, at home, or with friends, the lessons from these players will help guide you to success.

And don't forget, the story doesn't end here. Just like these athletes, you have the potential to overcome obstacles and achieve greatness in whatever you pursue. So keep working hard, stay positive, and always believe in yourself. The next great story could be yours.

As you close this book, I'd like to ask for your help. If you enjoyed these stories and found them inspiring, please ask your parents to leave a review on Amazon. Your feedback helps others discover the book and find their own inspiration. Plus, I'd love to hear how these stories have impacted you! I'm sure your favorite player would be interested to hear too, so why not send them a letter? You never know, you might get a response back, or at least a sticker or something cool from the team management!

Thanks for coming along with me on this journey through the lives of baseball's brightest stars. Keep on chasing your dreams, and remember, the sky's the limit when you believe in yourself. Play ball!

REFERENCES

Aaron Judge. (2024, July 27). Wikipedia. https://en.wikipedia.org/w/index.php?title=Aaron_Judge&oldid=1236890272

Acuna Jr., R. (n.d.). *Ronald Acuna Jr. quotes.* BrainyQuote. https://www.brainyquote.com/authors/ronald-acuna-jr-quotes

Adler, D. (2024, May 9). *Judge hits longest of year (473 feet!) in homestand full of deep drives.* MLB. https://www.mlb.com/news/aaron-judge-ties-mike-trout-for-longest-hr-2024?t=season-of-dreams-coverage

Adler, D. (2022, July 7). *The top moments of Scherzer's career.* MLB. https://www.mlb.com/news/max-scherzer-top-moments

Altuve, J. (n.d.). *Jose Altuve quotes.* BrainyQuote. https://docs.google.com/document/d/1m2ubCCSBpLOs_OsCrZRIdhDMDNuV9Ud_TF7V3pedWGk/edit

America's favorite pastime. (2018, March 14). National Archives. https://www.archives.gov/news/topics/baseball-and-the-archives

Angus, M. (2024, May 4). *Dodgers' Mookie Betts wins major award following dominant start to season.* Dodgers Nation. https://dodgersnation.com/dodgers-mookie-betts-wins-major-award-following-dominant-start-to-season/2024/05/04/

Arenado , N. (n.d.). *Nolan Arenado quotes.* https://www.brainyquote.com/quotes/nolan_arenado_1212180

Atlanta Braves first baseman highlights importance of skin and sun safety during melanoma awareness month. (2013, May 8). Melanoma Research Foundation. https://melanoma.org/news-press/atlanta-braves-first-baseman-highlights-importance-of-skin-and-sun-safety-during-melanoma-awareness-month/

Augustyn, A. (n.d.). *Shohei Ohtani.* Encyclopaedia Britannica. https://www.britannica.com/biography/Shohei-Ohtani

Barkan, R. (2023, August 6). *Baseball finally feels vital again.* Intelligencer. https://nymag.com/intelligencer/2023/08/major-league-baseball-finally-feels-vital-again.html

Bastian, J. (2024, February 28). *Bellinger, Cubs finalize 3-year deal.* MLB. https://www.mlb.com/news/cody-bellinger-cubs-deal-2024

Bellinger, C. (n.d.). *Cody Bellinger quotes.* BrainyQuote. https://www.brainyquote.com/quotes/cody_bellinger_1103804

Betts, M. (n.d.). *Top 10 Mookie Betts quotes.* BrainyQuote. https://www.brainyquote.com/lists/authors/top-10-mookie-betts-quotes

Bicks, E. (2019, October 23). *Juan soto: 5 fast facts you need to know*. Heavy. https://heavy.com/sports/2019/10/juan-soto-washington-nationals/

Bollinger, R. (2024, May 26). *Trout "feeling good" as he recovers from knee surgery*. MLB. https://www.mlb.com/news/mike-trout-gives-update-on-injury-recovery

Bowman, M. (2024, May 26). *Acuña has torn ACL, will miss rest of season*. MLB. https://www.mlb.com/news/ronald-acuna-jr-exits-game-vs-pirates

Bryce Harper. (2024, July 24). Wikipedia. https://en.wikipedia.org/w/index.php?title=Bryce_Harper&oldid=1236331863

Burns, G. (2019, August 23). Braves history: Ronald Acuna joins 30-30 club. *The Atlanta Journal-Constitution*. https://www.ajc.com/sports/baseball/braves-history-ronald-acuna-joins-club/4Pv01QWhHtGJEM1EY7qhvI/

Carpenter, M. (2024, June 24). *Rangers pitcher Max Scherzer makes impressive 2024 debut*. Yardbarker. https://www.yardbarker.com/mlb/articles/rangers_pitcher_max_scherzer_makes_impressive_2024_debut/s1_13132_40522754

Casella, P. (2024a, January 18). *Trout can play Hall of Famer leapfrog this year*. MLB. https://www.mlb.com/angels/news/mike-trout-in-reach-of-milestones-in-2024

Casella, P. (2024b, June 27). *Harper tops NL in Phase 1 of All-Star voting, earns starting nod*. MLB. https://www.mlb.com/news/bryce-harper-2024-nl-all-star-first-baseman

Cassavell, A. (n.d.). *Machado sharp in return to 3B: "It's so fun to watch him throw."* MLB.com. Retrieved July 27, 2024, from https://www.mlb.com/news/manny-machado-returns-to-third-base-after-surgery

Clayton Kershaw. (2024, July 25). Wikipedia. https://en.wikipedia.org/w/index.php?title=Clayton_Kershaw&oldid=1236660286

Cody Bellinger. (2024, July 13). Wikipedia. https://en.wikipedia.org/w/index.php?title=Cody_Bellinger&oldid=1234299784

Cole, G. (n.d.). *Gerrit Cole quotes*. BrainyQuote. https://www.brainyquote.com/quotes/gerrit_cole_1059880

Denton, J. (2024, February 16). *Arenado has "something to prove" for Cardinals in '24*. MLB. https://www.mlb.com/cardinals/news/nolan-arenado-making-changes-for-2024-cardinals-season

DiComo, A. (2024, January 11). *Alonso, Mets agree to deal worth $20.5M, avoid arbitration (source)*. MLB. https://www.mlb.com/news/pete-alonso-mets-agree-to-2024-contract-avoid-arbitration

DiGiovanni, S. (2024, June 3). *Bryce Harper wins NL May Player of the Month after explosive start to the season – Philly Sports*. Philly Sports Network. https://phillysportsnetwork.com/2024/06/03/bryce-harper-player-the-month/

Emotional Acuña grapples with 2nd ACL rehab, understanding the road ahead. (2024, May 30). MLB. https://www.mlb.com/news/ronald-acuna-jr-discusses-his-second-torn-acl-recovery

Footer, A. (2024, March 12). *Healthy and signed, Altuve ready for big '24*. MLB. https://www.mlb.com/astros/news/jose-altuve-hopes-for-healthy-season-after-new-astros-contract

Freddie Freeman. (2024, July 25). Wikipedia. https://en.wikipedia.org/w/index.php?title=Freddie_Freeman&oldid=1236520503

Freeman, F. (n.d.). *Freddie Freeman quotes*. BrainyQuote. https://www.brainyquote.com/quotes/freddie_freeman_781941

Frommer, F. (2024). Biography, baseball, Los Angeles Dodgers, first baseman, MVP, & facts. In *Encyclopædia Britannica*. https://www.britannica.com/biography/Freddie-Freeman

Gerrit Cole. (2024, July 26). Wikipedia. https://en.wikipedia.org/w/index.php?title=Gerrit_Cole&oldid=1236803750

Giancarlo Stanton. (2024, July 21). Wikipedia. https://en.wikipedia.org/w/index.php?title=Giancarlo_Stanton&oldid=1235852129

Giancarlo Stanton quotes. (n.d.). BrainyQuote. https://www.brainyquote.com/quotes/giancarlo_stanton_771652

Gomez, S. (2024, July 8). *Giancarlo Stanton's romance with Asiana Hung-Barnes: A swing and a miss*. HOLA!. https://www.hola.com/us/celebrities/20240708704993/giancarlo-stantons-romance-with-asiana-hung-barnes-a-swing-and-a-miss/

Harper tops NL in phase 1 of all-star voting, earns starting nod. (n.d.). MLB. Retrieved July 27, 2024, from https://www.mlb.com/news/bryce-harper-2024-nl-all-star-first-baseman

Harper, B. (n.d.). *Bryce Harper quotes*. BrainyQuote. https://www.brainyquote.com/authors/bryce-harper-quotes

Here are the hardest-hit home runs in MLB. (2020, March 13). *MLB*. https://www.mlb.com/news/hardest-hit-home-runs-in-mlb

Hoch, B. (2024, February 19). *Trimmer and more mobile, Stanton working to regain MVP form*. MLB. https://www.mlb.com/news/giancarlo-stanton-aims-to-regain-mvp-form-at-yankees-camp

Hoornstra, J. P. (2024, May 3). *Clayton Kershaw takes huge step towards return to Dodgers*. Dodgers Nation. https://dodgersnation.com/clayton-kershaw-takes-huge-step-towards-return-to-dodgers/2024/05/03/

"Iconic," "euphoric": Harper takes London by storm in opener. (n.d.). MLB. Retrieved July 27, 2024, from https://www.mlb.com/news/bryce-harper-leads-phillies-in-2024-london-series-opener

If these Vladdy quotes don't get Blue Jays fans fired up, nothing will. (n.d.). Daily Hive. Retrieved July 27, 2024, from https://dailyhive.com/vancouver/vladdy-guerrero-quotes-blue-jays-fans-fired-up

Infographic: America's favorite pastime - and barely anyone else's. (2023, March 30). Statista Daily Data. https://www.statista.com/chart/29617/popularity-of-baseball-in-selected-countries/

José Altuve. (2024). Wikipedia. https://en.wikipedia.org/w/index.php?title=Jos%C3%A9_Altuve&oldid=1236603158

Juan Soto. (2024a, January 12). Encyclopaedia Britannica. https://www.britannica.com/biography/Juan-Soto

Juan Soto. (2024b, July 25). Wikipedia. https://en.wikipedia.org/w/index.php?title=Juan_Soto&oldid=1236507784

Judge, A. (n.d.). *Aaron Judge quotes.* BrainyQuote. https://www.brainyquote.com/quotes/aaron_judge_948305

Justin Verlander. (2022, February 9). Wikipedia. https://en.wikipedia.org/wiki/Justin_Verlander

Kaneko, G. (2019, March 26). *Mike Trout is into sushi now, and more MLB food facts.* MLB. https://www.mlb.com/cut4/the-game-of-eating-smart-mlb-players-favorite-recipes

Kershaw, C. (n.d.). *Clayton Kershaw quotes.* BrainyQuote. https://www.brainyquote.com/quotes/clayton_kershaw_1061811

Ladson, B. (2024, June 20). *Cole returns to Yanks without skipping a beat, K's 5 in loss to O's.* MLB. https://www.mlb.com/news/gerrit-cole-returns-for-yankees-against-orioles

Landry, K. (2024, June 23). *Scherzer makes 2024 debut for Rangers.* MLB. https://www.mlb.com/rangers/news/max-scherzer-2024-debut-for-rangers

Langs, S. (2024, April 30). *Here is what's behind Soto's incredible start.* MLB. https://www.mlb.com/yankees/news/juan-soto-hot-start-to-2024-season

Latest MVP poll shows rare battle brewing in NL. (n.d.). MLB. Retrieved July 27, 2024, from https://www.mlb.com/news/juan-soto-mookie-betts-lead-second-2024-mvp-award-poll

Lemoncelli, J. (2024, May 30). *Yankees star Giancarlo Stanton's secret romance revealed.* New York Post. https://nypost.com/2024/05/30/sports/yankees-star-giancarlo-stantons-secret-romance-revealed/

Machado, M. (n.d.). *Manny Machado quotes.* BrainyQuote. https://www.brainyquote.com/authors/manny-machado-quotes

Manny Machado. (2024, July 24). Wikipedia. https://en.wikipedia.org/w/index.php?title=Manny_Machado&oldid=1236315767

Marcus Stroman. (2024, July 22). Wikipedia. https://en.wikipedia.org/w/index.php?title=Marcus_Stroman&oldid=1235955522

Matheson, K. (2024a, March 28). *Vlad Jr.'s 450-foot HR gives Blue Jays opening day jolt.* MLB. https://www.mlb.com/news/vladimir-guerrero-jr-450-foot-homer-blue-jays-opening-day-win

Matheson, K. (2024b, June 30). *Surging Guerrero vying to be AL's starting 1B in ASG.* MLB. https://www.mlb.com/news/vladimir-guerrero-jr-all-star-case-2024

Max Scherzer. (2024, July 25). Wikipedia. https://en.wikipedia.org/w/index.php?title=Max_Scherzer&oldid=1236660049

Mayes, W. (2024, June 13). *Arenado, Gray send Cardinals past Pirates.* Times Observer. https://www.timesobserver.com/sports/local-sports/2024/06/arenado-gray-send-cardinals-past-pirates/

McTaggart, B. (2024, March 5). *Verlander (shoulder) needs time to build strength, will open season on IL.* MLB. https://www.mlb.com/astros/news/justin-verlander-injured-list-to-start-2024-season

middledeer. (2021, August 12). *Pete Alonso's message to Mets fans: "Believe in us. And don't just believe. Know. ... Just smile, and know that we've got this."* Reddit. https://www.reddit.com/r/NewYorkMets/comments/p3a3ic/pete_alonsos_message_to_mets_fans_believe_in_us/

Mike Trout. (2024, July 23). Wikipedia. https://en.wikipedia.org/w/index.php?title=Mike_Trout&oldid=1236281317

Mike Trout injury update: Latest news on Angels star's timeline ahead of knee surgery. (2024, May 9). Sporting News. https://www.sportingnews.com/us/mlb/news/mike-trout-injury-update-news-angels-timeline-knee-surgery/b7b2cb07843ecb7429bf0b5a

Miller, S. (2024, January 31). *Mike Trout is fun: Fact.* Pebble Hunting. https://pebblehunting.substack.com/p/mike-trout-is-fun-fact

Minor, A. (2023, October 7). *17 fascinating facts about Bryce Harper.* Facts.net. https://facts.net/celebrity/17-fascinating-facts-about-bryce-harper/

Monagan, M. (2024, June 28). *This all-girls school received gloves from Ohtani -- and it made their year.* MLB. https://www.mlb.com/news/shohei-ohtani-donates-gloves-to-all-girls-school

Mookie Betts. (2024, July 27). Wikipedia. https://en.wikipedia.org/w/index.php?title=Mookie_Betts&oldid=1236877284

Moreno, M. (2024, June 24). *Clayton Kershaw News: Rehab assignment stopped.* MSN. https://www.msn.com/en-us/sports/mlb/clayton-kershaw-news-rehab-assignment-stopped/ar-BB1oOJJF

New York Yankees' Aaron Judge named starter at 2024 MLB all-star game. (2024, June 27). Sporting News. https://www.sportingnews.com/us/mlb/new-york-yankees/news/new-york-yankees-aaron-judge-starter-2024-mlb-all-star-game/b66896e8a03e9eb0d6bfbc1b

New York Yankees' Gerrit Cole official MLB return date revealed. (2024, June 17). Sporting News. https://www.sportingnews.com/us/mlb/new-york-yankees/news/new-york-yankees-gerrit-cole-mlb-return-date-revealed/640355d3211723368c72c213

9 benefits of playing baseball for kids. (n.d.). Sawyer Blog. https://www.hisawyer.com/blog/9-benefits-of-playing-baseball-for-kids

Nolan Arenado. (2024a, February 29). Encyclopaedia Britannica. https://www.britannica.com/biography/Nolan-Arenado

Nolan Arenado. (2024b, July 24). Wikipedia. https://en.wikipedia.org/w/index.php?title=Nolan_Arenado&oldid=1236313895

Nolan Arenado. (2024c, July 24). Wikipedia. https://en.wikipedia.org/w/index.php?title=Nolan_Arenado&oldid=1236313895

Nuamah, C. (2023, November 27). *100 interesting facts about Aaron Judge.* HubPages. https://howtheyplay.com/team-sports/100-interesting-facts-about-aaron-judge

Nye, J. (2023, October 14). *13 Mind-blowing facts about Vladimir Guerrero.* Facts.net. https://facts.net/celebrity/13-mind-blowing-facts-about-vladimir-guerrero/

119.9 mph! Stanton's huge HR the hardest hit in MLB this year. (2024, May 9). MLB. https://www.mlb.com/news/giancarlo-stanton-homers-on-hardest-hit-ball-of-2024

Ohtani, S. (n.d.). *I'm a student of the game, so I do feel like I need to grow every year, and I think I've been able to do that.* Quotes. Retrieved July 27, 2024, from https://www.quotes.net/citizen-quote/440175

Orfanides, E. (2017, July 10). *Giancarlo Stanton's family: 5 fast facts you need to know.* Heavy. https://heavy.com/sports/2017/07/giancarlo-stanton-family-ethnicity-parents-age-mike-siblings/

Pete Alonso. (2024, July 25). Wikipedia. https://en.wikipedia.org/w/index.php?title=Pete_Alonso&oldid=1236508180

Piccotti, T. (2023, March 22). *10 things you might not know about MLB superstar Shohei Ohtani.* Biography. https://www.biography.com/athletes/g43388193/shohei-ohtani-facts

Ronald Acuña Jr. (2024, July 21). Wikipedia. https://en.wikipedia.org/w/index.php?title=Ronald_Acu%C3%B1a_Jr.&oldid=1235763334

Sandler, T. (2020, October 14). *5 fun facts about Freddie Freeman.* Fangirl Sports Network. https://fgsn.com/5-fun-facts-about-freddie-freeman/

Sandler, T. (2023, July 12). *5 fun facts about Ronald Acuna Jr.* Fangirl Sports Network. https://fgsn.com/5-fun-facts-about-ronald-acuna-jr/

Scherzer, M. (n.d.). *Max Scherzer quotes.* BrainyQuote. https://www.brainyquote.com/quotes/max_scherzer_1053162

Selina. (2023, June 28). *15 facts about Freddie Freeman: The man on the plate.* Facts.net. https://facts.net/freddie-freeman-facts/

7 benefits of playing youth baseball. (2022, February 16). Stack. https://www.stack.com/a/7-benefits-of-playing-youth-baseball/

Shohei Ohtani. (2024, July 27). Wikipedia. https://en.wikipedia.org/w/index.php?title=Shohei_Ohtani&oldid=1236876336

Six things to know about Marcus Stroman. (n.d.). USA Baseball. Retrieved July 27, 2024, from https://www.usabaseball.com/news/six-things-to-know-about-marcus-stroman-306764322

Soto, J. (n.d.). *Juan Soto quotes*. BrainyQuote. https://www.brainyquote.com/quotes/juan_soto_1229501

Stearns: "I expect Pete to be the Opening Day first baseman." (2024, January 11). MLB. https://www.mlb.com/mets/news/pete-alonso-expected-to-stay-with-mets-entering-2024

10 days until spring training: Get your very own Marcus Stroman motivational quote. (2016, February 8). MLB. https://www.mlb.com/cut4/spring-training-countdown-get-your-own-marcus-stroman-quote-c163380530

10 things you didn't know about Mookie Betts. (2015, April 16). CBS Boston. https://www.cbsnews.com/boston/news/10-things-you-didnt-know-about-mookie-betts/

Top 15 quotes by Mike Trout. (2012). A-Z Quotes. https://www.azquotes.com/author/14806-Mike_Trout

Verlander doesn't miss a beat with quality start in '24 debut. (2024, April 19). MLB. https://www.mlb.com/news/justin-verlander-records-quality-start-in-2024-debut

Verlander, J. (n.d.). *Top 15 Quotes by Justin Verlander*. A-Z Quotes. Retrieved July 27, 2024, from https://www.azquotes.com/author/43074-Justin_Verlander

Vladimir Guerrero Jr. (2024, July 25). Wikipedia. https://en.wikipedia.org/w/index.php?title=Vladimir_Guerrero_Jr.&oldid=1236612991

Wells, A. (n.d.). *Bryce Harper, Phillies agree to record-breaking 13-year, $330 million contract*. Bleacher Report. https://bleacherreport.com/articles/2736846-bryce-harper-phillies-reportedly-agree-to-13-year-330-million-contract

Zuber, L. (2023, August 11). *43 facts about Justin Verlander*. Facts.net. https://facts.net/celebrity/43-facts-about-justin-verlander/

Made in the USA
Middletown, DE
12 December 2024